GUTS

A HEALTHCARE CEO'S BOLD BATTLE AGAINST STAGE 4 CANCER — AND YOUR HANDBOOK FOR HEALING

GUTS

A HEALTHCARE CEO'S BOLD BATTLE AGAINST STAGE 4 CANCER — AND YOUR HANDBOOK FOR HEALING

CHRIS GOLDSMITH

First edition – 2026

ISBN: 979-8-9945213-1-1

Produced in partnership with Kevin Johnson (kjbookcoach.com) and Richard Dodson (Richard-Dodson.com). Book cover and interior designed by Sue Luehring (sjldesign.carbonmade.com).

DEDICATION

To my three lovely ladies: My daughters, Emma and Jasmine, and my beloved wife, Jing. My sun rises and sets with you.

To Emma and Jasmine, you have already faced many challenges that will strengthen you for the road ahead.

To Jing, no word or phrase is sufficient to convey the love I feel for you.

TABLE OF CONTENTS

AUTHOR'S NOTE

I am not a doctor. Please do not consider anything in this book as medical advice. What I do bring is my experience as a CEO, President, COO, and multiple other senior roles within the healthcare system for the past 15-plus years. My roles have given me a unique privilege to see how the system works—and how it frequently doesn't work.

Once I received my cancer diagnosis, my wife and I jumped into action to heal my body. As part of this quest, I spoke to many cancer survivors as well as families in the middle of their fight. I realized there was knowledge I took for granted on how to heal our bodies that others didn't have. I also understand healthcare from the inside. These two realizations compelled me to write this book. I can't stand the thought of people sitting in a doctor's office, losing hope or suffering added frustration, finding their way through the maze of the current healthcare system.

I hope you gain two takeaways from this book:

1. **Hope.** Getting a serious cancer diagnosis doesn't have to be a death sentence. I and many others have found ways forward and you can too.

2. **Guidance.** Your hope can be empowered with insights into practical things you can do at each stage of the journey.

HOW TO USE THIS BOOK

The book is broken into three parts:

1. **A brief opening** that highlights your ability to fight back and take charge of your cancer journey.

2. **My story** and everything I went through to get here—physical, emotional, and spiritual—and the people who helped me.

3. **A concise "How-To" section** that gives my best thoughts on navigating each stage of healing your body (pre-diagnosis, diagnosis, and treatment).

While I believe there is much you can learn from my story, I fully recognize you might need the information in the how-to section of the book *right now*. I encourage you to use this book as a reference guide in whatever way works best for you. And please know I'm sending you PEP—prayers, energy, and positivity—as you work to heal your body.

PART 1: THE START

CHAPTER 1:

LIFE FALLS APART

Back when friends told me I was the picture of health, I couldn't help but agree. At age 46, I was in the best shape of my life. I routinely ran 10 miles at under an eight-minute pace. I performed weekly P90X workouts, some with maximum weights. I could even complete a workout called "the Murph," which entails running one mile, followed by 100 pull-ups, 200 push-ups, 300 squats, and another one-mile run, all in less than 45 minutes. Admittedly, I did the Murph without a weighted vest, but I impressed myself that I could do it at all.

As far as nutrition is concerned, I did far better than most people. My wife is an excellent cook, and Jing steadily moved our family of four to a mostly vegetarian diet. It happened to be that my two teenage daughters liked vegetables far more than pizza and fast food. Every year, our family ate less and less red meat and dairy, a healthy direction that came as an outcome of my wife's research.

A year later, everything had changed. After a sudden progression of disturbing physical symptoms, I found myself no longer at peak health. Far from it.

Not long after I turned 47, I received a devastating diagnosis that left me worried I might soon be dead.

MY MOM

My rapid decline came on the heels of a wrenching year for my family, a context if not a cause for my bewildering health challenges.

My mom had complained for years about various pains. When assorted specialists found "nothing wrong," she received a diagnosis of fibromyalgia. It felt like a junk conclusion, a convenient fallback for medical providers when nothing else was left. It was a problem without a treatment plan, and mom's lack of clear diagnosis meant Mayo Clinic rejected her for testing not once but twice over the years. Mom was active for her age, ate relatively well, and never smoked or drank. Outside of episodic pain, she seemed healthy.

Just a month after my 46th birthday, my family was pitching in to host my niece's wedding. That night, my dad phoned and said mom was incoherent and he had called 911. Although she was stable, doctors were running tests to determine if she had experienced a stroke. By the time I could see them the next morning, my mom didn't recognize me.

As dad and I sat in a dim hospital room and let mom sleep, we were told she was fortunate not to have suffered a stroke. But her brain MRI had unintentionally imaged her upper chest. The scan revealed a mass that most likely was cancer.

Time stopped. Cancer seemed unbearably worse than a potential stroke. Holding back tears at what felt like a death sentence, I shuffled away. I had to call mom's brother to break the news. Back in the room, my dad and I were mostly silent as the dreaded word "cancer" washed over and over us. In that moment, it felt like the most important thing we could do was listen to mom breathe. How else could we support her and reassure ourselves this would all be okay?

In another apparent diagnostic accident, an MRI of mom's chest scanned all the way to her pelvis. At her hip, the image revealed a six-inch mass. A biopsy confirmed that mom, a non-smoker, had stage-4 lung cancer with metastases throughout her body.

Only because doctors went looking for a stroke did they discover cancer. Really? How did previous doctors miss a problem a simple chest x-ray would have caught long ago? It's still unbelievable to me.

Throughout that summer, our family endured nonstop highs and lows. Exactly 90 days after that accidental discovery, mom passed.

I love you, mom.

MY WIFE'S DAD

My family didn't get much of a reprieve. A few months later, Jing's dad who was diagnosed with pulmonary fibrosis, stopped taking medications due to the side effects and started to decline. With no known cure, the condition is terminal. The person eventually suffocates to death, a path to dying I find terrifying. As my father-in-law declined, the only place he wanted to go was the casino, and my wife drove her parents there until he deteriorated to the point where he went on hospice at home.

His wife and Jing's sister were unequipped to care for him at home. Jing trained as an occupational therapist and was more at ease managing medications and attending to his daily needs, but long hours of caregiving left her exhausted. I'm not sure how she did it. In the end, a niece training to be a doctor stepped in for a long weekend. Shortly after, my father-in-law passed without pain.

Our two teenage daughters were blessed to never have witnessed disease or death, and in quick succession they lost two grandparents. What were they thinking? Were they okay? Were we providing enough support? My older daughter mostly kept her feelings to herself, and the younger read books for comfort. I was worried yet felt helpless in supporting them.

MY OWN BIZARRE ISSUES

As my 47th birthday neared, I began experiencing bizarre health problems. Pain in my non-dominant arm was diagnosed as frozen shoulder, an ailment known for striking victims of car crashes or diabetes. Neither was true of me.

The next week, on the last morning of a business trip, I awoke with intense neck pain. I literally cried while trying to eat breakfast. A lot of Advil got me home. I was diagnosed with neck torticollis, a condition

I thought only babies got. A week later, at mile six of a 10-mile run, my lungs, legs, and body simply couldn't go on. Dejected, I walked the four miles home.

A few weeks later, groin pain made going to the bathroom an agony. The urgent care provider said I likely had an enlarged prostate and told me to take a high dose of Aleve to reduce the swelling. It felt like the old "Take two and call me in the morning."

I started to wonder if I was somehow really messed up, but my primary care provider (PCP) was the last place I wanted to turn for help. At my previous annual physical, without looking up from his perfunctory poking and prodding, he asked how I had been. I told him my mom had died. He mumbled "Sorry to hear that" and asked me to inhale, continuing his protocol as quickly as possible. I concluded he didn't give two shits about me, and it was clear he would offer little help in my current state. So I found a concierge doctor who would partner with me to get to the bottom of whatever was wrong.

I was still experiencing bouts of pain, and sleeping was becoming more and more difficult. My new PCP indeed gave me the time and attention that felt like every doctor should offer. She ordered a battery of blood work and other diagnostic tests. Unfortunately, the results were unsettling. All my liver levels were elevated, and an ultrasound showed spots on my liver. An MRI was scheduled.

I was in back-to-back video meetings when my PCP called with results that changed my life.

The MRI found a mass the size of a potato above my bladder and several spots on my liver. She said I had a very rare form of bladder cancer that had metastasized to my liver.

Less than a year after my mom's accidental diagnosis, I had gone from peak health to a diagnosis of Stage 4 cancer. My insides churned with all the same things every cancer patient thinks and feels. But the first question that popped into my brain was if I like my mom had only 90 days to live?

WHY THIS BOOK

This book is my effort to help more humans. I want to make a positive dent in the universe.

I put my training as an engineer to use in the first part of my career when I worked as a software and strategic consultant. In my early thirties, I made my way in healthcare, and a light bulb went off. If I could create a better business framework, physicians could focus on providing patients with better care.

I had found purpose for my existence! With this North Star in mind, I went on to lead healthcare businesses with annual revenues ranging from hundreds of millions to multiple billions of dollars. I held fancy positions like CEO, COO, President, and Senior Vice President.

Many of these businesses could point to amazing success stories of helping patients through dire times. These real-life results fueled my desire to work harder and harder to help more and more humans, yet we could only help a fraction of patients. Countless more continued to suffer without getting the help they needed.

My professional and deeply personal interactions with the healthcare system have given me an intimate knowledge of what works in the systemand where it is curse-at-the-world broken.

I want to share what I have learned.

WHY GUTS?

I chose GUTS as my title because GUTS is exactly what it takes to overcome your diagnosis. Your diagnosis likely feels like an anchor roped around your feet, dragging you underwater as you gasp for breath. In this dire situation, you need GUTS to realize you have agency. You need GUTS to question experts. You need GUTS to potentially not follow the pleadings of family members and friends. You need GUTS to make the final decision on your treatment plan and not automatically defer that decision to a white coat.

As we continue to learn about the human body, we're starting to realize the vast power of all that plumbing in our abdomens. Our GUTS contain 100 trillion bacteria—some good, some bad. Some people even call it our second brain. I firmly believe in the mind-body connection, the more you listen to your body, the more it will tell you exactly what it needs. As I went through my journey and encountered doubt and indecision, I trusted my GUTS. Are you willing to trust your intuition—your own GUTS?

And why GUTS—for me specifically? It was in my GUTS that my whole life was turned upside down. It's where the diagnosis grew and spread undetected for months. It's where I stuffed emotions and memories I didn't want to feel or recall. My GUTS changed my life.

As an aside, GUTS was my favorite penny poker game as a kid. I played with my grandpa and grandma at any holiday gathering. I always hoped the pot would get to a dollar and I would win.

Unfortunately, we aren't playing for pennies anymore. Your life is at stake. Are you in? Do you have the GUTS?

CHAPTER 2:

DIAGNOSIS ISN'T DESTINY

I believe in data, a conviction I discovered as part of my wiring as an engineer. Now in my role as a healthcare leader, I count on data to guide my decisions. Unfortunately, the numbers say cancer has a high likelihood of impacting us as individuals or the people we love.

The bare facts about cancer are only the beginning of the story. We can let the numbers scare us or we can use data positively and proactively to strengthen our resolve. To choose the best path forward. Even to bring about breakthroughs that otherwise might not happen.

When you hear the dreaded "Big C" word, it's crucial to understand there is much that remains within your control.

There's no minimizing the threat of cancer, and its mere mention can cause us to freeze. Let's face a few big-picture numbers, then deliberately move ahead.

- CDC data for 2020 reported 1.6 million new cancer cases, with 602,000 Americans passing annually.
- For every 100,000 Americans, 403 were diagnosed with cancer, and 144 passed.

- Of the 403, nearly 300 diagnoses (74%) were one of the "big four" cancers: breast, prostrate, lung, and colon/rectum.
- Yet, of the 144 who passed, only 82 (57%) were caused by the big four.

This last fact isn't surprising. A much greater proportion of funding goes into detecting and treating the top four cancers, which has resulted in increased life expectancies for people diagnosed with one of these common forms.

According to American Cancer Society research, men have a 40.9% lifetime probability of being diagnosed with cancer, and women have a 39.1% probability. The good news is overall mortality has decreased steadily in the United States due to reductions in smoking and increased screening of breast, colorectal and colon cancers. However, the trend is less encouraging worldwide.

- In 2022, there were 20 million new cancer cases and 9.7 million deaths, totals expected to increase by 50% by the year 2040 to a predicted 29.9 million cases and 15.3 million deaths.

Also concerning is the increasing rate of early-onset cancers, defined as a diagnosis in adults between the ages of 18 and 49.

- In a recent study, early-onset cases increased 79% and deaths increased 27.7% from 1990 to 2019.

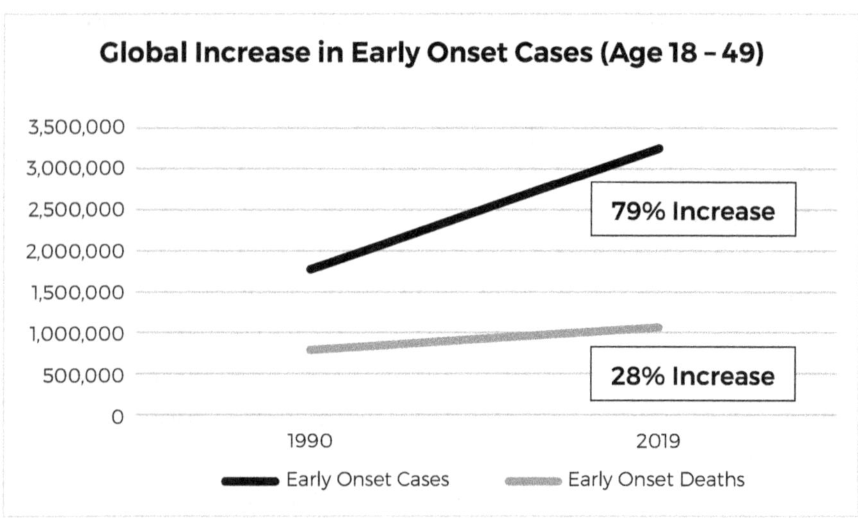

Unfortunately, the US has the highest rate of early-onset cancers in the world at 282 per 100,000.

The cancer risk faced by couples puts cancer risk in stark terms. If you are in a relationship:

- The chance **neither** of you will get cancer: only 36%
- The chance **one of you** will get cancer: 48%
- The chance **both of you** will be diagnosed: 16%

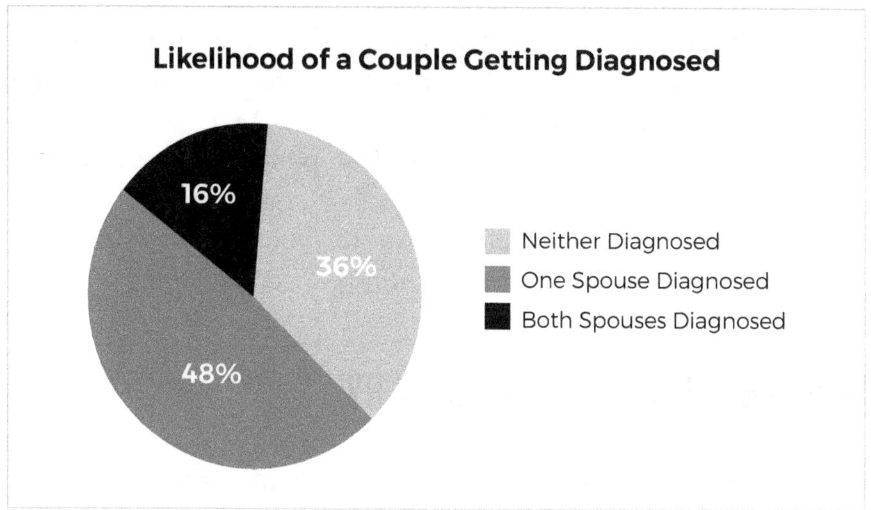

HOPE AHEAD

Those are difficult numbers to process. But there's far more to the story. If you or someone you love just got a life-changing diagnosis, I invite you to take a moment to regroup.

Pause.
Take a deep breath.
Slowly exhale.
Consider one crucial fact:
Every single day,
many people learn they have been healed
from a cancer diagnosis.

A few encouraging statistics:

- From 1991 to 2016, overall US death rates from cancer **declined 27%.**

- Lung cancer: The **long-term survival rate has tripled** for one of the most common cancers in the world thanks to daily immune checkpoint inhibitors for people with small cell lung cancer. In fact, a woman in the UK was the first to receive a vaccine for lung cancer. Who would have thought a vaccine for cancer was possible?
- Skin cancer: Melanoma is one of the deadliest skin cancers. However, the use of immune checkpoint inhibitors has **increased life expectancy by years** for many.
- Most relevant to all of us, **countless people diagnosed with cancer find their way to remission.** Go to radicalremission.com—especially the healing stories page—to learn about humans who are thriving after a range of daunting cancer diagnoses.

YOUR DIAGNOSIS ISN'T YOUR DESTINY

I often discourage people newly diagnosed with cancer from learning about their prognosis, which Oxford defines as "the likely course of a disease or ailment." Why? Because a prognosis is merely a statistical prediction and a "typical scenario" or "likely course" for a particular type or stage of cancer often raises mental, emotional, and physical roadblocks to what might be possible. As my oncologist told me, "No one is average." What he meant is people usually fall far short or long of the average when it comes to how long they live after a diagnosis. In statistical terms, this is called "fat tails."

These "fat tails" matter to every cancer patient because every human is unique. In fact, I constantly remind myself that I am an "N of 1," which in statistical language means there is no one else like me.

You are also an N of 1. Your age, diet, exercise, genetics, epigenetics (gene expression), environment, mental health, and more all play a part in why you received the diagnosis. They can also play a critical part in your process of healing. In other words, you aren't a statistic. You are a one-of-a-kind story.

Your diagnosis isn't your destiny.
You can't control your diagnosis,

but you can decide what to do about it.

Your uniqueness introduces important factors to your path to illness and your healing journey. But one thing matters more than anything in determining the outcome. The most important factor in your healing is your mindset.

DRIVER OR PASSENGER?

You are about to go on a metaphorical road trip filled with twists, turns, breakdowns, surprises, and moments of sadness, beauty and laughter. You can lean back in the passenger seat and close your eyes to what awaits you around the next corner. Or you can grab the wheel and do your best to influence the route.

- Do you want to be a passenger during your treatment plan, following along with whatever the physician says? Or
- Do you want input from the experts within the bounds of their specialties yet ultimately decide what to do?

When my mom was diagnosed with stage 4 cancer, we encouraged her to take small steps that could improve her wellbeing, like drinking a healthy smoothie. As much as we tried, she wouldn't engage. She was a passenger on the journey, and we had precious little time with her after the diagnosis.

You must answer one core question yourself:

Are you the driver or a passenger?

Deciding to take the wheel requires courage. The process of making active decisions creates energetic conversations and can even cause conflict. Staying alert and steering can be exhausting. But deciding to be the driver can make all the difference in your outcomes.

You can tell I have a strong bias here, both in my capacity as a healthcare professional and in my response to my own diagnosis. I want to drive. After all, this is my body. This is my life. How can I leave important decisions to someone else?

Depending on the pace of your illness and the amount of pain and other challenges you face, it might be difficult for you to manage discussions with physicians. If this is your situation, you can still choose the driver mindset and involve a loved one or friend to assist and advocate for you by asking important questions so you can jointly decide what is best.

Throughout your cancer journey, your response to this driver-passenger question is crucial. Do you believe you have agency over how your journey plays out? Will you exercise that power at every possible turn? Are you willing to make tough choices and changes?

I WANT TO LIVE

If you or a loved one are facing a cancer diagnosis, the best moment to act is always now.

I have met people so discouraged by their illness that they wonder about giving up. So what motivated me to fight my cancer?

Quite simply, I want so badly to live. I have so much more to see, do, learn, and love. I want to see what impact our two amazing daughters create in the universe. I long to witness their major life events. I would not willingly leave my wife to the possibility of long decades of being alone.

Beyond my family, I felt I had more to give. I believe I am a force for good in this world and can make a greater positive dent in it. That is a significant part of the reason I am writing this book. Can I use what I have experienced to help other humans? That is my goal as long as God gives me the strength to be on this planet!

Most people do not necessarily reach the point of giving up. But they surrender responsibility to physicians in white lab coats. At first glance, it indeed feels like we have little control. Cancer showed up out of the blue—and what can we do? We might say, "The doctors are the experts. It's their job to save me." We may think, "I'm at the mercy of the system. I sure hope they heal me. They are going to tell me what to do and I'm going to do it and then we see if it works—or not."

True, physicians are the experts. To a degree. They know sickness.

They studied what Western medicine says is state-of-the-art.

Unfortunately, many physicians are too busy or burnt out to track the latest developments across all types of cancer. They generally abdicate when it comes to anything outside their refined expertise which means they don't often consider the role in healing of emotional health, diet, exercise, supplements, non-traditional treatments, and more.

If you are reading this book, I want you to believe you have agency over decisions and over improving your likelihood of survival. I believe you indeed have significant agency:

1. You can accept the recommended treatment plan or opt for a different approach. Yes, there will be immense pressure from physicians, your family, and friends, but this is your body and your life. Make the decision you feel is right, and don't acquiesce and die on account of politeness!
2. You can decide to make changes to your diet.
3. You can decide if you want to adjust your approach to exercise.
4. You can decide to address potential emotional issues from your past.
5. You can decide your mindset and how you are going to think.
6. You can decide to adopt mindfulness practices such as meditation or prayer.
7. You can decide if there are ways to reduce stress in your life.
8. You can decide if you want to explore alternative therapies like intravenous vitamin C, acupuncture, reiki, Ayervedic approaches, or others.
9. You can decide to explore natural supplements that could boost your immune system.
10. You can decide to explore off-label drug use as another low-cost way to treat your body.
11. You can decide how to breathe. As silly as it sounds, I focused on changing my breathing. Several times a day, an alarm on my phone reminds me to pause just to breathe. My daughters laugh. I say, "More belly, more better!"

To have our best shot at recovery, I think all of us need to care for the whole body, mind, and spirit.

For some people, the pain of cancer and ensuing treatments is too much to bear, especially if they believe there is no possibility of improvement. Even if you are in that tough circumstance, I want you to assert your agency and dignity, two values American healthcare often takes from us. I invite you to adopt the words of the Serenity Prayer:

> ***God, grant me the serenity to***
> ***accept the things I cannot change,***
> ***the courage to change the things I can,***
> ***and the wisdom to know the difference.***

CHAPTER 3:

TAKE YOUR POWER BACK!

Since my own diagnosis, I have spoken to dozens of people and family members where cancer or another serious medical condition has put their lives at risk. In listening to their questions, I realized there was so much they didn't know about how the system works.

My goals with this book are simple:

1. **Give hope:** I will let you in on my deeply personal journey as I struggle to heal my body, mind, and spirit from a rare Stage 4 cancer diagnosis. I tried to document transparently everything I went through, including details about a humiliatingly public psychotic event. I did this to show that no matter how broken you feel, you can still become whole again.

2. **Give guidance:** If you're reading this, either you or someone close to you is likely facing a cancer diagnosis. I'm sorry you're going through this. No one decides to "get" cancer, and I want to empower you to reclaim your agency. You can take actions that can prove decisive in healing body, mind, and spirit for you or your loved one. The second part of this book relays my recommendations on crucial points to consider for each step in the cancer journey. I intentionally made this section succinct so you can quickly access the content most helpful to you at the moment.

The cancer journey takes place in a world of out-of-control and often incomprehensible healthcare costs. I want to help you not only resolve your health concerns but also prevent financial calamities and pay as little out of pocket as possible. My suggestions also help you navigate getting a "no" on coverage and how you could potentially turn that into a "yes."

I want to help you along this journey, and I believe the best way I can do that is to speak transparently about my own experiences, good and bad, so you can use that information to chart your own path forward. Think of my story as one more data source for you to consider as you make your own decisions.

If you don't have time at this point in your journey to read my story of hope, then I recommend you go directly to the "How-To" section of the book for my practical advice.

The How-To portion contains my personal and professional perspective on things you can do to navigate the road ahead. Time is the most valuable thing we have, so I have intentionally made this section concise, raising awareness of potential approaches. Where a suggestion resonates with you, I often recommend further resources to propel you forward.

This book is divided into three sections. You or a loved one might choose to read it straight through, or you can turn to the section you need right now. Here are the contents:

This introduction to the book is the portion you are now completing.

I explain what I was thinking and feeling during my diagnosis and treatment so you understand you aren't alone. I describe the unexpected mental and emotional trauma I experienced and how I recovered. And I share takeaways—my insights into myself and their importance for my future.

PART 3: YOUR HOW-TO GUIDE (Page 141)
I offer my practical insider's guide to the healthcare system and getting the help you need. I summarize my thoughts after my own remission and encourage you to stay the course in your own healing.

I have already let you in on the basics of my diagnosis. There is so much more to my story—and yours. I never saw cancer coming, and I certainly never anticipated how it would remake my life for the better.

TAKE YOUR POWER BACK

Let's talk heart-to-heart. We might become the driver and do all these things and still not get the results we hope for. While this could fill us with disappointment and even rage, we can take solace in the fact that we did our utmost. Just realizing how much we can control can be comforting.

I am not a doctor. None of my recommendations should be taken as medical advice. I am simply an engineer who has worked across our healthcare system with extreme attention to detail and partnered with my loving wife, a research ninja on all things health.

Why listen to me? Given we live in an age of disinformation, you are right to ask. Wherever possible, I link directly to clinical studies in PubMed, which houses the National Institutes of Health research database, or to leading Cancer Centers of Excellence. At the end of it, you must do what you feel is right for your body, and I would encourage that above all else.

I am so sorry we have met this way. I wish you or your loved one wasn't suffering from this terrible illness.

Now is the time to act.
In the words of Rage Against the Machine,
"We gotta take the power back!"

PART 2: MY JOURNEY

CHAPTER 4:
SOMETHING IS VERY WRONG

The weeks leading up to my cancer diagnosis felt like I was tumbling down a rocky running trail.

As I experienced these strange symptoms one after another, I began to wonder if something was seriously wrong.

First came the pain in my left shoulder, which I mentioned at the start. I assumed it was a simple muscle strain. Like most dedicated exercisers, I continued my workouts, trusting it would fade. The persistent pain finally drove me to see my primary care physician, who referred me to an orthopedic specialist. A few tests and scans confirmed I had frozen shoulder of my non-dominant arm, which required an injection and potentially a year of physical therapy. Not only was the recovery timeline disheartening, but the diagnosis was also perplexing.

Next was the neck pain so extreme it brought me to tears. Another trip to an orthopedist, which seemed like the obvious place for that kind of problem. I was a fitness guy, right? My mind came up with all kinds of explanations for the pain, but neck torticollis wasn't one of them. The muscle relaxant they gave me was unbelievably strong. The pill knocked me out for the weekend, and not until Sunday evening could I keep my eyes open.

These issues had forced me to skip a couple of my usual long weekend runs of 8 to 10 miles, and I was eager to get back to my rhythm. In preparation for the run, I made sure I got a full night of sleep. Out on the trail, I was surprised to be surrounded by others doing a 5K race. I felt elated as spectators cheered me on and the official photographer snapped my picture. But a little more than halfway through the run, shortly after turning toward home, I couldn't breathe. My whole body hurt. I normally try to push through, but this felt different. I had to quit running and walk the remaining miles home. I felt dejected that my hard-won cardio fitness had seemingly instantly vanished.

There had been other random symptoms. My father-in-law's pulmonary fibrosis had declined rapidly after Chinese New Year, and he had decided to go on home hospice. As we arranged a hospital bed and television in his living room, I bent down to pick up a chair and shouted at an intense pain in my groin. This happened again while moving furniture, and the acute pain seemed highly specific to different movements. The next day, I went to urgent care, where I was tested for kidney stones. When that came back negative, they surmised I had an enlarged prostate and recommended I take a lot of Aleve to reduce the pain and swelling.

Over the past year, I had gone to this urgent care multiple times with bizarre pains.

Almost inevitably, the healthcare providers in urgent care recommended I take over-the-counter pain medication and not worry about my pains.

None of this felt like proper care. There was no curiosity about my random symptoms or repeated visits. People seemed to just want to get to the next patient.

I became convinced I needed someone who cared about me enough to find out what was actually going on, and this was when I located a new primary care physician (PCP) through a concierge program. I paid an annual fee in exchange for more access to my doctor and supporting team, an option I was blessed to be able to afford. What previously felt like an indulgent expense now felt like a necessity.

The doctor could see me on my 47th birthday. While the timing wasn't ideal, she was amazing. She instantly ordered a full battery of bloodwork. The nurse who took my blood was concerned that my veins would hold up for nine vials, and they just barely made it. The results indicated all my liver levels were elevated. A subsequent ultrasound found spots on my liver that my doctor wanted to get a better look at, but at this point, my worries were serious but surmountable. It's quite common to have non-cancerous spots on your liver. Or so I believed.

THE MRI PRIOR AUTHORIZATION

Given the elevated blood levels and spots on my liver, my PCP ordered an MRI (magnetic resonance imaging) of my torso and pelvis to occur one week later. That should be as simple as showing up and lying in a tube, right? Not so. Any expensive test typically requires your health plan's prior authorization, or "prior auth," to ensure that their own doctors believe the test is medically necessary.

Yes, health plans also employ doctors, with the intent of avoiding the expense of unwarranted tests. As I would discover, ensuring that a prior authorization goes through—and on time—requires calling people at each step of the process. I phoned my health plan, and the nurse on the other end informed me it could take up to 10 days for them to review and approve or deny my doctor's order. My test was only seven days away, and their failure to approve it in time would cause my appointment to be canceled and pushed back, pending their approval. Through several escalations up a chain of call-center supervisors, I explained repeatedly that the delay was unacceptable and that my MRI was approved prior to my scheduled appointment. This would become a recurring theme for us. Unfortunately, it's likely to be one for you too, if you find yourself in a similar situation.

The scan occurred early one morning, followed by a day packed with meetings. As I was in my gown preparing to get on the table, I asked how long the test would take. Two or three hours. I had no idea an MRI could take that long! I texted my team that I would be missing more meetings than I thought.

The technicians said they would scan my torso and pelvis first without contrast. A radiologist would read the results live to determine if contrast dye should be injected. After over an hour inside the tube, I was pulled out and told that the radiologist wanted contrast. The techs also asked if I had ever been on dialysis. Their question startled me. Dialysis is for people with kidney failure, a very serious condition. Why ask that?

As I was in the MRI tube with dye flowing through my body, I started to really worry. I let myself cry a little while trying to hold still.

I still believed that if something was seriously wrong with me, at least we would catch it early. I'm in amazing shape, so how could they find anything truly bad?

THE NEWS

Our pre-scheduled summer plans were in full motion. While our older daughter was in California at a two-week course researching cancer cells, my wife and younger daughter had planned a mother-daughter getaway to the Boundary Waters in northern Minnesota. On the Friday of the MRI, I was completely alone. Since my wife would be driving most of the day and cell phone coverage would be spotty at best, we agreed to wait to talk until that evening after they reached their destination. I assured Jing it was 95% likely the spots were benign, 4% something like fatty liver, and 1% something awful (cancer).

I had looked it up. I trusted the data. I told myself I was okay.

After the MRI, I headed home and hopped on a Zoom call. Besides my family being away, my PCP was also off for her daughter's graduation. During one of my meetings, I received a cell call from "Unknown." I ignored the unidentified call and went back to my meeting. However, a few minutes later, "Unknown" vibrated again. I resisted the temptation to answer but saw a message pop up. My PCP had broken away from her vacation to call me. I freaked out and told others on my call I needed to drop. Immediately. I dialed my PCP's office so they could reach back to her. By now, I was shaking.

Within minutes, my PCP called and walked me through the terrible news. She described the potato-sized mass directly above my bladder and fifteen spots on my liver, likely cells spread from the bladder tumor. She believed the source of the metastases was the urachus, a tube from the belly button to the bladder. It usually disappears after birth, but in rare cases a tumor later grows from it. How rare? Bladder cancers make up only 4% of all cancers, and urachal cancer is less than 1% of all bladder cancers. That translates to 0.01-0.02% of all cancers. I was very unlucky indeed, and my doctor was extremely sorry.

It was late morning. I was stunned. And I had no one to talk to.

My wife and daughter would be on the road for several more hours. A few close friends knew I was getting scanned, but I didn't want to talk to them before speaking with Jing. My dad lives across the street, and eventually I walked over. He was meeting with the grief counselor he had been seeing since my mom passed and would stop by later. I had no urge to search online for details of my condition. Given its rarity, I knew I was unlikely to find anything encouraging. So I went to my basement where I keep several large tropical fish. I hung out with my fish friends and turned my focus to building a complex Lego set, a hobby that helps me relax.

What is anyone supposed to do when they hear they have cancer?

Having never been in this situation, how the hell should I know what to do? I did what brings me peace, watching my fish swim back and forth and building Lego.

When my dad showed up, I asked him to sit down. We made typical chitchat, then I told him the sobering news. He looked like he was in shock. I remember him saying, "I'm really sorry to hear that, Christopher." He asked a few questions, we hugged, and he left. Alone again, I watched the hours slowly roll by into late afternoon. I called a dear friend, an anesthesiologist specializing in critical care. He cried when I shared what my PCP told me. I asked him not to tell me about the prognosis for urachal cancer, but his reaction communicated that it wasn't good. I was grateful when he guided me through breaking the news to my wife.

While anxious to speak to Jing, I felt bad I was about to ruin their trip. My youngest had been looking forward to her adventure in the Boundary Waters, and they had just started. Eventually, around 5pm, I got a text that they were checked into their fun cabin room for the night before paddling into the wilderness. Their voices were cheery and excited. Following my friend's advice, I asked my wife to sit down and made her promise she wouldn't drive for at least an hour. Once she agreed, I told her the news. It was the hardest phone conversation I have ever experienced. With our younger daughter in the room, Jing tried hard to hold it together, But both our girls are super perceptive, and there was no avoiding our daughter realizing something bad was happening. I apologized for not being there and that Jing would need to tell her the news.

The scene still brings me to tears. My wife was crying profusely. I felt helpless not being there to comfort her. After untold minutes of crying, I recommended they stay put and come home in the morning. My suggestion made all the sense in the world to me because they had just finished driving all afternoon. Once we hung up, I sat on the couch and cried. One thought rampaged through my mind:

How much time do I have before I'm dead?

CHAPTER 5:

WHAT NOW?

My dad texted to ask if I wanted to grab something to eat at a nearby BBQ restaurant. He ordered a sandwich and a beer. I just got a sandwich. He said I should get a beer—heck, we should go for ice cream too. Never mind that I don't like ice cream. I had completely stopped drinking alcohol more than a month before when my bizarre health issues started. Now hardly seemed like the time to drink up.

I recalled that when my mom was sick, my wife and I tried to get her to consider changing her diet. Jing had researched the benefits of plant-based diets for people with cancer. At one point during my mom's journey, my wife said, "If you ever get cancer, the first thing we're going to do is become vegan." Her words would prove prophetic.

Jing texted that they wanted to see me that night, and they were starting the five-hour drive. When I returned home after dinner, I called two of my closest friends. I didn't really know what to say other than the facts presented to me. I asked if they had any ideas about what someone should do after learning they had cancer. I was still struggling for ideas, so I went back to building Lego.

In those first moments,
I didn't feel anything.
Not anger.
Not even sadness.

I just felt numb.

I recalled the saying "Laughter is the best medicine"—so I decided to watch a funny movie. Evidently someone had "borrowed" the DVD of my favorite comedy, *Old School*, so I settled on *Wedding Crashers*. I laughed a little, cried a little, and by the end of the movie my wife and daughter had arrived home. I held them both as we all cried and cried.

I awoke the next morning to negative thoughts permeating my brain. Our older daughter was a high school senior, and the younger a freshman. Will I know where my older daughter gets into college? Will I see either girl graduate from college—or even high school? From the little information I had, it seemed unlikely I would get to walk our daughters down the aisle, so I didn't even ask the question. What about another Christmas, six months away? Will I ever take another trip with friends?

When my wife woke, she instantly broke down. She said she couldn't even look at me without crying. My heart shattered. Nothing I could do to provide a salve for this pain. It was unrelenting, and it was hurting the people I loved most.

Our oldest daughter was scheduled to be at the cancer research camp for another week. The experience had already erupted into a minor crisis. The professor wasn't showing up, and our 17-year-old and her peers were outraged that the teaching assistant had scheduled daily "nap time" for them. We had debated whether our daughter should come home, but after the professor intervened, she chose to finish the program. We again decided to let her stay and tell her my news when she arrived home. I dreaded the conversation only slightly less than telling my wife. Once she was back home, we told her and the floodgates of sorrow and dread had immediately returned. At least we were done hiding the facts.

THE IMMEDIATE AFTERMATH

Because I work in healthcare, I am blessed to count several physicians as close friends. Three of them—and one non-doctor—became my medical advisors, people I would call or text after every appointment. I began asking for their advice, and given that I live in Minnesota, our attention immediately turned to getting an appointment at Mayo Clinic, a world-renowned center of excellence for cancer treatment.

That request, however, isn't as easy as saying, "I have a rare cancer. Give me an appointment." There is a multi-step process for submitting all your information. Someone within Mayo's opaque, layered infrastructure will decide whether the clinic will grant you an appointment. I knew the process from watching my dad try multiple times to obtain an appointment for my mom, but she was always rejected. Even with this less-than-happy history, I felt I had no option but to start the process.

I was president of a national healthcare company focused on caring for the sickest-of-the-sick Medicaid members, people with low income who cannot afford health care. These humans had largely been forgotten by the traditional health care system, and we tried to provide white glove concierge care to restore their mental and physical health. To properly fight my own illness, I knew I needed to step away from work and give healing my sole attention.

I worked with the CEO to construct a new organizational structure that could function both in the near future and in the event I never returned, another sobering thought. I addressed the executive leadership team and my own team the following Monday. In a tearful goodbye, I urged them to continue the mission of the company and help as many disadvantaged humans as possible get the care they need. I personally asked them for what I called "PEP."

PEP—PRAYERS, ENERGY, AND POSITIVITY

While I am a very private person, something inside me told me that I needed to look outward for help. I intuitively knew I would need a lot of humans to help me if I was going to survive this diagnosis. Even so, I didn't want anyone to feel sorry for me. While I was very young to be diagnosed with this rare cancer, I also recognized I had enjoyed a life that was more than a little blessed up until that point.

I received my initial diagnosis on a Friday morning, and just a couple of days later, an idea popped into my head. This kind of flash of inspiration would happen repeatedly on my journey.

> ***What I needed was PEP:***
> ***Prayers, Energy, and Positivity.***

I suddenly knew I needed as much PEP as people were willing to give. I'm religious, but not everyone is. I couldn't afford to exclude anyone willing to help lift me up. So from non-religious humans, I asked for energy and positivity. From the religious, I would happily accept their prayers.

One of my classmates from my MBA program sent me the following note: "I am in Italy with my wife for her friend's wedding. I'm not Catholic or even very religious, but I prayed for you at a lovely church in Polignano al Mare. Thinking of you and wishing you lots of positive energy."

I teared up reading the note. Look at what he was willing to do for me. A non-Catholic, non-religious person entering a church and saying a prayer for little old me. That was an amazing dose of PEP from across the pond. It helped move me into and keep me in such a positive state of mind—how could I not heal my body with so much positivity coming my way?

FIRST STEPS

While I reached out to everyone I knew in the medical field for advice, my wife was true to her word. She instantly converted me to a vegan diet, avoiding any food derived from animals. As context, I am a slow eater, and chewing salad takes me an eternity. On top of that, I never really ate vegetables until we got married. The massive salads Jing made would take me an hour to consume. Honestly I felt like a little kid at dinner—as in "You can't leave the table until you eat your peas!" To help ease the burden of consuming so many vegetables, my wife started juicing fresh and frozen produce. She ultimately found a machine that presses vegetables to extract maximum nutrients.

One of the first things I heard when I shared my diagnosis became a powerful truth: "Attitude is everything!"

I took my friend's words to heart and began putting sticky notes on my bathroom mirror. The notes greeted me first thing each morning, and the positive affirmation wall grew over time with letters, prayers, and cards.

How was I feeling? Not great. I had abdominal pain and nausea. I found eating was a challenge. Moreover, any slight movement the wrong way could cause shooting pain, which impacted my sleep. I stacked up so many pillows in bed that I was almost sitting up, which made sleeping even more difficult.

My PCP referred us to a local oncologist, who was highly recommended by other patients. I had chosen to carefully guard the information I took in, so Jing did all the research in preparation for my first appointment. She came loaded with questions and pressed for clarifications. We both took copious notes.

The oncologist took a large panel of bloodwork, a practice that became standard procedure at subsequent appointments. He also ordered a biopsy of a liver spot to confirm the diagnosis. Concerningly, my liver levels were even more elevated from the check my PCP performed just a few weeks prior. My medical advisors debated whether the biopsy should examine the liver spots or the suspected primary tumor above my bladder, but ultimately the oncologist chose to biopsy a liver spot.

The biopsy the following week involved a tiny incision to retrieve a sample. Once again, the prior authorization process put the test at risk and required my direct intervention to get permission for this essential fact-finding. When I woke up from the anesthesia, my side screamed with intense pain. I didn't realize they had given me a very strong painkiller intravenously, but I needed more! Eventually I was able to stand, dress, and make it home. Once there, I mostly slept for the next two days, completely wiped out by that tiny incision.

Online medical portals usually give patients access to test results before an opportunity to speak to a doctor. Jing and I opened the results expecting it to confirm urachal cancer, but it stated a new type of cancer—GIST, a gastrointestinal stromal tumor.

What? Was this different cancer better? Or was it worse? In keeping with our approach. I again talked to my medical advisors while my wife dug in online. I was careful not to ask my advisors about the prognosis, but I immediately sensed this was a "better" cancer—if there is such a thing. Jing's research seemed to corroborate this.

The MRI had definitively identified the cancer as urachal, and the biopsy had definitively identified the liver spot as GIST. Which was it? While extremely rare, it also raised the possibility of two primaries, having not one but two cancers at the same time. It was a dire potential diagnosis that I tried to ignore. My medical advisors split 50/50 on which cancer it was.

Thankfully, no one really believed I had two cancers. But we had to wait to find out.

CHAPTER 6:
FEAR OF MISSING OUT

While all these events were playing out, I worked feverishly in the background to try and get an appointment at the Mayo Clinic.

I thought renowned clinics like Mayo had secret protocols, best practices, and additional treatments available nowhere else. When I was first diagnosed, I therefore expended almost all my energy attempting to get an appointment at one of these centers. I thought it would make all the difference in my healing.

We all have a fear of missing out,
and FOMO only becomes worse
when your life hangs in the balance.

I was grateful to have national insurance coverage that allowed me to access physicians regarded as the best in the world. Yet in hindsight, I left each visit completely depressed, frequently with my wife or me or both in tears. My quest to access these resources offered limited additional insights, and any additional bits of knowledge came at a huge emotional toll.

For starters, something as simple as creating a Mayo account online requires an identification number granted by a doctor at Mayo. Fortunately, one of my medical advisors was friends with a Mayo doctor. While this doctor wasn't an oncologist, the ID number he provided meant I could register for a urology account and be granted this mythical Mayo account number. This number allowed me to BEGIN my dialogue with a Mayo nurse who clearly channeled Gandalf's character in *The Lord of the Rings* with her "You shall not pass" during every interaction.

The MRI and biopsy already performed by my hometown providers weren't good enough for Mayo, which required one of its own doctors to evaluate the actual tissue samples to confirm the previous doctor had done the work correctly.

I can appreciate a desire for accuracy, but I discovered later that my health system had a partnership with Mayo. If there was any uncertainty, they do not render a result. They defer to Mayo and send it off to let them provide the diagnosis. My local doctors had not felt the need to forward anything out to Mayo. It felt like the real reason for redoing the analysis was so Mayo could bill my insurance. Again.

The gatekeeper nurse said that once Mayo receives the original tissues, their doctors will retest the sample, review the result, and then decide whether to accept my case. If they accept it—a big if—I would be allowed to schedule an appointment.

"How long will all of this take?" I asked.

"One or two weeks to get the sample," she replied. "One week to get the results. Another few days to determine if Mayo will accept your case. Then three or four weeks for the next available appointment."

I don't know what cancer I have, so I cannot begin treatment. At best, it was at least a month and a half before I could potentially speak to a Mayo doctor. My head was exploding as she told me this.

PUSHING FOR MORE

Not to be deterred, I talked to anyone I knew who could accelerate getting an appointment at Mayo. I also wanted to see Mayo's best expert. After speaking to several physicians across the country, they independently recommended the same doctor.

Fine. But how do I get to him? A doctor friend of a doctor's friend knew the specific oncologist and reached out to him and explained my case. He agreed to see me and gave me a date and time for an appointment. Given my determination to get an appointment—and the feeling that the normal process was like running into a brick wall—this was thrilling news.

One problem. My schedule on the Mayo online portal didn't show the appointment.

A call to Mayo reassured me that the appointment time and date were real, so on a Monday morning, my wife and I made the two-hour drive south to Rochester. As I sat in the clinic's atrium that day trying to eat a little lunch, my nausea was especially bad. It required every ounce of mental focus to swallow without throwing up. I was overwhelmed by the swarm of sick people and their caregivers. It felt like an airport concourse. While I was ecstatic to be seeing a national expert on my cancer, I was bewildered by the memory of being at Mayo on a business trip just a year earlier—and now, being a patient.

How did I become so sick
that I needed all this?

My wife and I rode the elevator up to the oncology floor, and I went to the desk to check in. It should have been a formality. But I wasn't on the doctor's schedule. I frantically texted my friend who texted his friend to ask what the heck was going on. I began to panic. How could we go through all this effort with dozens of phone calls and texts and a two-hour drive only to be told I do not have an appointment?

The desk person asked me to sit down. Jing and I sat. Waited. Paced. Waited. Eventually, they called me back to the desk and said something to the effect that "He wasn't planning to see you, but since you're here, he will make time." I was too relieved to be annoyed. I was just happy the answer was yes.

THE CLINIC VISIT

The nurse called us back and her first words were "Congratulations on getting into Mayo!" She was more correct than she realized. But isn't Mayo a world-renowned center of excellence dealing with the toughest and rarest cases on earth? Shouldn't they be trying to help people like me?

Before I could see the doctor, I saw a younger doctor doing a fellowship with Mayo. I spent more time with the fellow than the Mayo physician, who went through everything about my case, so the Mayo doctor was fully briefed on all our questions.

I had already coordinated the release of my tissue sample to Mayo so they could re-run the biopsy, and I had confirmed that Mayo received the tissue sample. It should have been rendered that previous Friday, but it was not. Even as we drove to the clinic, we checked if the results had come in. They had not.

We meet with the Mayo doctor said by everyone in my network to be the person I need to talk to. He reasonably explains that he is still waiting for the biopsy results, so we cannot finalize a treatment plan. But he believed I had urachal cancer and went on to describe its treatment. I would get a port installed in my chest. I would receive traditional chemotherapy. There was a good chance my body would not tolerate that chemotherapy, or it would be ineffective on my cancer. If that is the case, we will try another chemotherapy until...

The rest was unspoken, but it was clear I would be dead if we got to that point.

My wife and I asked if therapies exist other than the blunt instrument of chemo that had been around for more than 50 years. Had Western medicine not come up with anything better?

No. Given the rarity of urachal cancer. Nothing.

Understandably, little research is done on treating such a rarity. Effort and dollars go into the top five cancers: skin, breast, lung, prostate and colorectal. Essentially, that was it. He had nothing to add. He noted that I do not need to return to Mayo because I can just get the chemotherapy drug administered by my local oncologist to save me the drive.

It felt like the doctor was sending me home to die.

Our drive home started quietly. I think Jing and I were both in shock. We expended so much effort to get to this appointment, almost didn't get it, and when we finally spoke to the foremost expert in the field, we learned that not much could be done for me.

During the drive, we got the alert that the Mayo biopsy results were in. We decided not to open the results until we arrived home.

At home, we opened the portal, and the Mayo pathologist agreed that the biopsy indicated GIST rather than urachal cancer. Our optimism grew upon being diagnosed with this stage 4 cancer rather than the other. We had missed getting the results by just a few hours; getting them earlier might have changed our entire discussion.

GIST

This diagnosis and forthcoming genetic sequencing would mean the treatment protocol for my cancer was straightforward. I realized my FOMO was unwarranted.

I met with my local oncologist a few days later. He believed the tumors were indeed GIST but recommended we confirm with a CT (computed tomography) scan. If the diagnosis was confirmed, genetic tests on my biopsy tissue would determine whether I was a match for the most common form of treatment—the drug Imatinib, which is the generic version of Gleevec.

It would take a few weeks before we knew the results. And it took hours of effort and days of waiting for a pre-auth for the CT scan.

The scan was far faster than an MRI. Instead of lying in a tube for hours, it was over in a few minutes. The scan largely confirmed what we already knew, but it did find four additional tumors in my intestines. So while it confirmed the cancer hadn't spread to any other parts of my body, we felt deflated to see the total tumor count increase to 20.

While the certainty of diagnosis was reassuring, my blood levels were not. My liver levels had continued to increase at a staggering rate, meaning the organ was not functioning well. During the most recent bloodwork, some of my liver levels were 400% above the normal range. Just 30 days earlier, they were only 40% above normal range.

I was already wasting no time pursuing a diagnosis and treatment. Now it felt like I was in a day-by-day race against time.

CHAPTER 7:

GO EAST, YOUNG MAN

My choice to combine the best of Western medicine with Eastern and non-traditional medicine was driven by the belief that our broader society has lost or forgotten things people have understood for hundreds if not thousands of years.

In evaluating non-Western treatments, I sought to weigh the promised benefits against the expense of the treatment and its potential side effects.

In other words, to pursue a specific approach I had to believe the risk was worth the reward. In the how-to section of this book I add detail about a process for evaluating possible treatments.

IV VITAMIN C THERAPY

Intravenous (IV) therapy to load my body with vitamin C was one of the first non-traditional treatments I tried. Advocates of the treatment say cancer cells mistake vitamin C for glucose, their primary food source, and the vitamin C ingested by cells proves toxic and causes them to die.

Western Medicine regards this approach as ineffective, a position reinforced by the mixed results of a Mayo Clinic double-blind study. Advocates point out that research used oral rather than IV vitamin C and say patients can't absorb enough oral vitamin C to kill cancer cells. After weighing the evidence, the logic of the treatment still made sense to me, and my medical advisor team didn't see a downside to trying it. I felt like the more ways we could attack the cancer cells, the better.

Interestingly, many non-traditional clinics provide IV vitamin C and some offer treatment at home. Because I wasn't feeling great, we opted for an at-home IV. We were lucky that a highly personable nurse trained at the Cleveland Clinic was administering the IV. Before starting, she tested my glucose to establish a baseline level to ensure I was getting enough vitamin C, but not more than my body could handle. The whole process took about an hour. Afterward, I felt like my skin was full or squishy, and I had less pain and slightly more energy during the rest of the day.

I received this therapy a few times at home, but it's expensive, costing over $200 per visit. So we consulted an integrative medicine doctor for a cheaper in-clinic option. I completed an incredibly long intake of details including poop and gas, followed by a thorough visit with the doctor who drew many vials of blood to check levels usually ignored by mainstream medicine.

While the visit was helpful, I didn't feel a connection with the doctor. Moreover, when I tried in-clinic vitamin C therapy, the nurse failed to find an obvious vein and had to poke at the other side. A few minutes after the IV started, the bag blew a connector and I had to yell for the nurse to come back and fix it.

The ordeal made my incredible nausea even worse, and it took all my focus to not vomit. I left shaking and struggling to walk to the car. In that moment, I wondered if this was a foreshadowing of the rest of my life, trading one type of pain for another. The nurse badly colored my experience, and I never wanted to go back.

I chose to continue receiving therapy at home. But there was more to consider.

We heard so much negative

feedback about IV vitamin C from Western physicians that our family dinner table erupted in a debate about whether I should continue at all.

The medical establishment outside the US is generally more open to non-traditional treatments. I went to business school in France, so I reached out to my international business school classmates for referrals to physicians in their home countries, and several classmates connected me directly or relayed my questions. I hoped for a friendly audience with more support for this practice, but the doctors, like their US counterparts, strongly recommended I cease the therapy, concerned it could inhibit the chemo drug I was taking. Given this, we decided to stop IV vitamin C. For now.

ACUPUNCTURE AND MORE

I mentioned earlier that I had never tried acupuncture, partly because I honestly wondered what getting stuck with needles could possibly accomplish. It made no sense to me. But given my diagnosis, I was willing to try.

The practitioner who inserted the needles also connected me to a TENS (Transcutaneous Electrical Nerve Stimulation) device that passed an electrical current into my abdomen. Every other visit, she added headphones to push ozone into my ears to improve my mental clarity. I went with it even though I had no sense of my own mental fuzziness. Maybe everyone else did.

The fact that I came home smelling awful made my family hate the ozone treatment. The worst was a full-body ozone treatment where I was zipped into a plastic bag from my neck down. Jing came along to see this for herself. Ozone high in the earth's atmosphere protects humans from damaging ultraviolet rays from the sun but inhaling it can be irritating and cause lung damage, so the whole approach felt sketchy. We began questioning if we should find another acupuncturist, and we later moved to the acupuncturist who has been a trusted ally through the twists and turns of my journey.

After reading *Radical Remission* by Kelly Turner – a book I highly recommend for anyone dealing with a cancer diagnosis – we connected with an acupuncturist in San Francisco. Because of the distance, he was initially hesitant to meet with us. We completed another lengthy intake form, and our effort resulted in a two-hour call with him that hit us like a blast of fresh air. This practitioner knew more about the cancer and the latest research than the multiple oncologists I had met with. He described the specific cellular processes the cancer uses to mutate and how I should alter my routine by not overdoing exercise. He noted that some of the leading research comes from China because they spend a significant amount of money researching GIST due to the simple fact that they have more absolute cases.

This practitioner told me patients need to know why they are trying an approach. What outcome do they expect? If that result isn't met, what should they adjust?

Whether acupuncture, supplements, or another tactic, treatments should be undertaken with full engagement of our critical thinking skills. The acupuncturist was driven by facts and hypotheses, which resonated with me. He acknowledged that IV Vitamin C can help, but for the time and money, a trip to Hawaii surrounded by nature might be even more beneficial. I finished the appointment with an initial supplement regimen and a recommendation that I find an acupuncturist close to home so I could incorporate that practice into my weekly routine. He would advise from afar but only if the local acupuncturist could relay the goals and outcomes of various treatment protocols.

I felt like I had found my head coach for Eastern Medicine. However, I still needed to find my quarterback to run the plays and call an audible when needed. The solution coalesced as Jing and I interviewed multiple acupuncturists. The conversations were fascinating, and ultimately, we found an amazing practitioner just minutes from our house. In breaking with the football analogy, she happened to be the acupuncturist for the Minnesota Twins baseball team. I loved that we always started our sessions by talking about how I was feeling and what had happened that week. In addition to guiding the treatment, she advised me on what to do or eat, or avoid, during the next week.

I felt like I had found my talk therapist before I even knew I needed one.

REIKI ENERGY HEALING

I had never heard of Reiki, "a Japanese technique for stress reduction and relaxation that also promotes healing. It is administered by 'laying on hands' and is based on the idea that an unseen 'life force energy' flows through us and is what causes us to be alive" (reiki.org)."

I was highly skeptical. Reiki seemed really out there. But others reported favorable results from the practice.

How should I assess a good Reiki healer? Like most people, I started with proximity to our home and found a licensed healer nearby. She operated out of her condo, with a bedroom converted into a Reiki room, which is essentially a massage table with dim lighting and an air diffuser where I picked my preferred scent for each session – lemon mist.

During sessions, I simply closed my eyes and breathed deeply while she placed her hands on various parts of my body, a touch even lighter than the lightest massage. I saw some colors in my mind but nothing else noteworthy. After the first session, the healer said my intestinal area was "very dense," which indicated a lack of movement. But she didn't feel anything was "blocked," a positive. My wife asked how it went. I didn't really know. The session was pleasing, but I didn't really feel anything.

The next morning, much to my surprise, I jolted wide awake just after 6am. For context, between my meds and the weight of everything going on, I typically slept until 9am or significantly later. I was so alert I got up and ticked off a bunch of tasks before the rest of the family woke from their summer break slumber. I thought, "Wow! What's different?" Only the Reiki healing performed the preceding day.

I went back a few more times and never again experienced that early morning burst, but the healer said the energy around my intestines continued to move, which I took as a positive. In subsequent sessions, she always instructed me to pull a card from a deck that offered a message to me. This felt like crossing the line between psychic and palm reading, which didn't resonate with me. It was likely due to this shift and the fact that I couldn't feel anything that I didn't incorporate Reiki into my ongoing regimen.

MEDITATION

As part of my journey into Eastern Medicine, I wanted to learn more about meditation but didn't know where to start. I had never attempted to meditate. I turned to my LinkedIn community for recommendations and tried multiple phone apps.

I set aside time immediately after waking to test a variety of meditations. At first, my mind would wander off within minutes of starting. Not at all the intense, positive focus I hoped for. Friends said this was common for beginners and told me to stick with it. My mind still felt like a pinball ricocheting from thought to thought.

I concluded that I needed to start with shorter meditations. Anything longer than 10 or 15 minutes was too much for me, and I found Insight Timer to be more helpful than well-known apps like Calm, Headspace, and Waking Up. I specifically liked Giovanni Dienstmann's track "What Meditation Type is Best for You," a guided tour of nine varieties of meditation, which became my roadmap to understanding my options.

Even before the diagnosis, I had used the Bas Rutten Breathing O2 Trainer, a mouth device for building lung capacity. That background was helpful in attempting the breathing techniques of various meditation styles. I knew that breathing is critical for sports performance, and I discovered that different breath rhythms can induce everything from calm to feeling high.

One breath I eventually incorporated into my meditation was Kapalbhati pranayama, which involves rapidly contracting and releasing the abdomen to force out air. Also called the "breath of fire," its goal is to generate heat. I found it useful after I quieted my body and wanted to activate it for the specific purpose of killing cancer cells.

After attempting these different breathing techniques, I realized I was a bad breather.

I had an unhealthy habit of breathing shallow all day long, rarely taking a deep breath until lying down at night. I needed to relearn how to breathe.

I realized I lived on high alert. This constant fight-or-flight mode never gave my body a chance to recover, even when I slept. I frequently awoke in the middle of the night with my brain flipped on, inevitably thinking about work. I ran incessant mental scenarios of how I should have executed better or how I could manage an upcoming challenge. It often took hours to turn off my brain. It's a wonder my body didn't crash long before my 47th birthday.

After much trial and error, two approaches to meditation really resonated with me: Wayne Dyer's "Morning Ah" and Drea Palmer's "Cancer Meditation." Wayne Dyer focuses on positive manifestations and what we want to be true. Drea Palmer, a cancer survivor, leads visualizations of destroying cancer cells and generating stem cells to repair the body. I was already doing similar visualization on my own, but Palmer's level of detail felt exceptionally effective. For months, I diligently ensured this meditation was my first act every morning. For at least two hours after waking, I set aside my cell phone and everything else to focus completely on my healing.

A friend asked how I reconcile meditation with my Christian faith. I replied that integrating the two practices simply feels natural. Praying after meditating seems like the perfect way to close a session.

I felt so great afterward that sticking to this discipline became easy. The positive energy set the table for the rest of my day, and I felt like I was becoming more whole in mind, body, and spirit. Visualizing my cancer spots shrinking and disappearing helped create an expectation that I could be healed. Many people with a cancer diagnosis don't actually believe that, but I sure as hell did.

I need to make a clear disclaimer about meditation. This part of my story gets complicated.

As helpful as meditation was to me, I was unaware of its risks. As I will describe in later chapters, my intense approach to meditation nearly killed me.

If you have never meditated, don't begin without understanding the potential dangers. Start slow, and if at any point you feel dysregulated—not yourself—then stop!

CHAPTER 8:

THIEVES OF HOPE

Even as we pursued multiple non-traditional approaches to healing, we didn't relent in maximizing Western Medicine.

Just 15 days after starting chemotherapy, my liver levels had dropped from 200-400% above normal to the middle of the acceptable range. Wow! Clearly, Imatinib was working. While my medical advisors cautioned me not to read too much into a blood test, we were nevertheless ecstatic. I was feeling the PEP!

While these liver blood markers were excellent, my kidney blood marker was going in the opposite direction. My creatinine had become so significantly elevated that my numbers met some of the criteria for chronic kidney disease, the precursor to kidney failure.

The prospect of needing dialysis absolutely terrified me. If the Imatinib was really damaging my kidneys, I told Jing I would rather quit the drug and take my chances than be tethered to a dialysis machine for the rest of my life. It wasn't the quality of life I wanted.

Facing such a frightening choice, I wanted a clear answer. Are my kidneys fine or are they on the path to failing? It felt like a simple question relevant to many patients on chemo.

Past bloodwork revealed my creatinine level had always been borderline high, and prior to my diagnosis I heard Dr. Peter Attia say on a podcast that creatinine is a poor test for assessing kidney function. It is always too high or too low, depending on body type. Dr. Attia recommended cystatin C as the superior blood marker. Luckily, before my diagnosis I had pushed my primary care doctor to check that marker, and after some discussion, she reluctantly agreed. The initial test showed normal kidney function. When I convinced my oncologist to repeat the cystatin C test, it came back nearly identical to the earlier test.

In other words, my kidneys were fine. Or were they?

Just to be sure, I sought to verify which test is the true indicator of kidney function. I reached out to physicians I had seen at two centers of excellence. One had never heard of the cystatin C marker and told me to trust the Creatinine measure instead. Another punted and referred me to a nephrologist – a kidney doctor. I was dumbfounded. Shouldn't the people treating cancer be experts on tests to assess the health of impacted organs?

After literally 15 minutes of Google searching, Jing and I found that the National Kidney Association in the US acknowledges creatinine is less expensive and more widely available but recommends providers transition to testing for cystatin C. Moreover, the UK's National Institute for Health and Care Excellence recommends cystatin C. The experts refused to comment on this point, but we found credible sources in mere minutes.

Unbelievable. Had I not heard the podcast and followed up with research, I would still be wondering if I had to quit a cancer drug or face a life on dialysis.

ON THE HOOK FOR AN ENORMOUS BILL?

The treatment protocol for GIST implied I would take Imatinib until the day I die. My gut says less medicine is better, and I wanted to see if oncologists agreed. We also wanted to know how much progress I needed to demonstrate to make surgical removal of my tumors an option.

While I had already started the intake process with the MD Anderson Cancer Center at the University of Texas, I didn't have a specific physician I wanted to see. When my friend's oncologist agreed to see me, she became the obvious choice. As part of the intake, the clinic requested my biopsy slides so MD Anderson could have their own pathologist review. My local health system and Mayo had already validated the results, but that wasn't good enough.

The voice on the phone put me on a recording so I could promise aloud that if my insurance didn't cover the cost of reading the slides, I was responsible for payment, which was anywhere from $800 to more than $4,000 per slide. I assumed my biopsy involved one or two slides. A lot of money but within reach.

I asked how many slides they needed to review. "Nearly 30." Quick math told me the clinic wanted me to sign off on a potential $100K liability!

My head exploded. I uttered words I won't write here.

My health insurance had been great up to this point. They fully covered Mayo's second opinion on the slides, but I was highly doubtful they would pay for a third. I was so desperate I was willing to risk it, but how could the average American with less than $5,000 in savings even take that chance?

This feels like extreme waste. As a healthcare executive, I see two possibilities. Institutions don't trust work done by others, and/or they want the revenue from additional tests. Surely it should be possible for centers of excellence and others to recognize test centers that meet specific criteria so expensive work isn't repeated. When I pressed them on this, they cited outlier case(s) where they found something that Sloan Kettering or some other famous institution missed. I really wonder how often that happens?

I was feeling great, other than the potentially staggering financial obligation. I was no longer nauseous, and my abdominal pain was totally gone. My liver numbers dropping to normal told me the drug was working. With those facts in hand, combined with my daily meditations, I couldn't have been in a more optimistic mindset. I was eager to talk to MD Anderson and see what's next.

Jing and I arrived on a steamy summer Houston evening the night before my appointment and attempted to walk around a little before we melted. The next morning I planned to work out, but we received a call that the oncologist could see us early if we were available. I scrapped my workout, and we rushed over to navigate the maze of medical buildings and find the right elevator up to her office.

THE APPOINTMENT

The oncologist was nice, but her news was not. Given the expense of the trip and our pressing desire for answers, my wife and I had an extensive list of topics to cover. The first question: Do I really need to be on this drug for the rest of my life? My friend was no longer taking it. Could I get to a point I didn't need it?

The doctor was insistent.
I needed the drug as long as I
lived or until it stopped working,
typically one year.

What? A year? I had just spoken to a woman on it for more than 20. That's the number I had in my mind, not 365 days. The oncologist said that in most patients, GIST mutates after nine to 15 months, rendering the drug useless.

My wife and I were exceptionally careful about dividing our research responsibilities. Jing understood in detail all the treatment options, the hierarchy of drugs, and their corresponding side effects. I just knew a sequence of three drugs was available. If one stopped working, I would take the next. While it was encouraging that my cancer had multiple drugs when some cancers have only one, I knew that progressing down the chain meant a declining quality of life.

The doctor confirmed Jing's research. My head spun. I had less than a year of feeling good before needing a different drug with worse side effects. And then that would stop working. And then I would need another drug with even more debilitating side effects. And then I was done. I was speeding along a downward journey where each month would likely be worse than the last until I died.

I was getting beyond sad and upset.

We switched the subject to surgery. If the drug will rapidly stop working, the sooner we do surgery the better, right? The doctor's response was as blunt as her last: With cancer in so many spots, the surgery would be far too risky, and the likelihood spots would be missed was far too high. Don't even think about surgery.

Undeterred, I asked a question I employ all the time as a healthcare executive, "What would need to be true for (fill in the blank) to happen?" In this case, the blank was surgery. The oncologist flatly refused to answer. My wife and I each rephrased our questions, but no matter how we asked, the doctor wouldn't give us a goal to shoot for. It was simply,

"You're not at a place to ever think about surgery." Dread was setting in. I was trapped in a shrinking maze, and every turn took me to another dead end.

To further depress our mood, the doctors said going forward that MRIs were my only choice because the dye used would be less toxic to my kidneys than a CT scan. She cautioned against taking Advil or Tylenol because they also cause kidney damage. "We need to keep your kidneys healthy for as long as possible," she said, "given they appear to be on the road to failure."

So now I need to worry about my kidneys just as much as my cancer? Yes.

We asked for her opinion on IV vitamin C treatment; she was equally negative. Without citing proof, she ventured that it could inhibit Imatinib and strongly recommended against it.

We were grasping for any hope. Is there a clinical trial anywhere that might make sense for me? No. Nothing is appropriate for you at this stage of your treatment. Keep taking the Imatinib until it quits working.

I felt like the oncologist gave me a death sentence numbered in months, not years.

Our last line of questioning got personal. Doesn't it matter that I'm decades younger than the average person diagnosed with GIST? That I'm in great physical shape? That I had gone completely vegan? While she acknowledged these as positive attributes in my favor, she was unwilling to change her timelines.

How does none of that matter? Why couldn't I be different?

We quit asking questions, fearing the doctor might divulge yet another new horror we weren't prepared to deal with.

My wife and I walked back to our hotel without saying anything. We collapsed in the hotel room, and I started to cry. My worries and negative thoughts from the early days of my diagnosis came rushing back, except with an even briefer timeline. Will I be able to take our older daughter to college a year from now? Will I even see where our high school freshman goes to college? Maybe I should shut down and sell my huge aquarium while I still can so my wife doesn't have to deal with it.

Time seemed to be slipping through my fingers. My wife implored me not to give up. While I nodded in agreement, it all felt rather hopeless. The anvil of death was hanging over my head and could drop and crush me at any moment. We packed up and sullenly traveled back to Minnesota.

MORE OF THE SAME AT MAYO

After the MD Anderson ordeal, my optimism took a severe hit. My local oncologist recommended a second opinion at Mayo, even though my first experience wasn't positive. I thought, *why not*?

We opted for a video visit rather than drive down again. At the appointment, I felt like Bill Murray in *Groundhog Day*. Same thing over and over. The young oncologist echoed the answers at MD Anderson. We were beginning to feel that surgery was my only shot at a longer life, so we pushed that issue. Like the other oncologists, the Mayo doctor evaded the question, "What would need to be true?" We were discouraged but unsurprised. Extending a glimmer of hope was a prescription they apparently were trained to never write.

The only silver lining was a referral to a Mayo Integrative Medicine physician. Although we had met with an independent integrative doctor, we still needed a guide for non-traditional therapies and supplements.

THOUGHTS ON CENTERS OF EXCELLENCE

I was blessed to be able to go to not one but two of America's best centers of excellence for cancer care, an opportunity beyond the reach of most Americans. Yet I had never felt more hopeless. After each of these appointments, it took days to emotionally recover. I slept a lot and let myself cry in secret.

These doctors understand their specific area better than anyone else in the world. Yet as their specialization continues to advance, their ability to understand anything outside that specialty continues to decrease exponentially, I would argue.

It feels as if their goal isn't to heal but to provide the most technically accurate information about an individual diagnosis and prognosis with no allowance for anything the data doesn't give them 100% certainty to say. Maybe that's what they should do. Avoid giving false hope because that is not the answer either.

On the one hand, my family can appreciate this point of view. Caution is a prudent choice. The oncologists who saw my mom on hospital rounds during her cancer journey gave wildly varying assessments of her future. One said, "You'll have lots of tests this summer, but you aren't going to die." My mom was gone 90 days after the diagnosis.

On the other hand, there is so much about each human outside the box of a standard diagnosis. Outcomes can depend on an individual's diet, physical fitness, emotional well-being, family support, ability to manage stress, and more. Every person measures differently on each component, yet doctors won't acknowledge how those factors might help or hurt what's happening "inside the box" of a diagnosis.

Admittedly, I've thought a lot about this, and there's no easy way for doctors to handle it. What troubled me most was their reluctance to offer any kind of goal or target—no matter how improbable—for me to aim toward. We've all seen remarkable comebacks in sports, those Hail Marys and walk-off home runs; I just wanted to know what that might look like for me. Without it, there wasn't much to anchor my hope to.

I have asked myself countless times why these experts are unwilling to think, act, or advise outside the box. Are they burned out? Is their training to blame? Does the healthcare system extinguish their curiosity?

Every doctor would offer a different set of answers. Yet as someone who works every day with physicians, I believe multiple factors got us to this place:

1. **Training.** Physicians receive little or no training on considerations like emotional health, nutrition, or exercise and their impact on a human's overall health.

2. **COVID.** The pandemic was incredibly difficult for healthcare professionals across the country, and I'm not sure that people and the systems they work within have emotionally recovered. Doctors were always a revered profession, but for the first time ever, their work was politicized, and in some circles, they became public enemies.

3. **Risk of Malpractice.** Doctors are at risk every day they show up to work. They can be sued by any patient who thinks they made a mistake. Why risk going outside the box if it might cost you? The American Medical Association offers context, revealing that 2017 malpractice insurance premiums for obstetricians/gynecologists ranged from $49,804 to $214,999, often varying with geography. Other specialists have lower annual premiums, but this is a real expense to the doctor and the entire healthcare system.

4. **Financial Productivity.** The financial engine of healthcare demands physicians see more patients in less time to meet their targets for wRVU (work relative value units). This is how most fee-for-service (FFS) institutions judge whether their doctors are

productive enough to justify their salaries or potential bonuses. While I'm oversimplifying – quality metrics are also included – but doctors who don't see "enough" patients are at best marginalized, or worse, pushed out.

These factors have left many doctors stressed and exhausted, feeling that their job is just a job. Along the way, they lose their true north of why they became a doctor in the first place.

My local oncologist breaks this mold. He is middle-aged, so he doesn't exhibit youthful exuberance untempered by painfully difficult cases. He has possibly observed more prognoses than the physicians at centers of excellence. In my appointments, he and I discuss with complete openness all the non-traditional things I'm trying. Although he acknowledges his background doesn't equip him to weigh in on their efficacy, he still supports me in trying them. He doesn't judge. He doesn't draw the hard lines I have seen in other oncologists.

The effectiveness of his care is more than his supportive bedside manner. I have thought hard to identify this factor, and it's this: My doctor treated me like a whole human trying to have a life outside of this terrible diagnosis. After we debriefed my visits elsewhere, he acknowledged the statistics I heard. They were accurate. But he also said,

"You need to live your life and plan for the optimistic case rather than always worrying about the pessimistic case."

That mindset has made all the difference.

I genuinely hope my experiences at centers of excellence are the exception and that other patients receive outstanding care. While I know several people who haven't, I also know many who have. Nevertheless, for me these centers of excellence are where my hope went to die. Hope is one of the best prescriptions we can get, and that is why I refer to the centers, not the doctors, as the "thieves of hope."

CHAPTER 9:

A DAY IN THE LIFE OF A CANCER PATIENT

While I have described the dramatic key points in my journey since my diagnosis, I want to give a sense of my average day after a few months.

> ***Overall, I felt blessed in the extreme. While I had occasional odd episodic pain, I feel minimal day-to-day discomfort.***

The chemotherapy side effects are mostly limited to fatigue, inability to do intense workouts, eyelids with a slight droop, lips cracking with dryness, muscle cramping and my skin being more sensitive to cuts and scrapes. Many others have much more severe side effects from the same drug; I attribute my mild side effects to everything else I am doing to keep my body healthy.

Still on leave from work to fully dedicate my energies to healing myself, I nevertheless tried to follow a structured schedule. I attempted to get up by 8 or 9am, but if I felt tired, I went back to bed. Sleeping was the most important thing I could do to help my body heal. Doing the Morning Ah and Cancer Meditation described above took about an hour, followed by exercise. That was another hour, depending on the workout. I ate my morning oatmeal, and while it cooled I worked on my lung capacity with the Bas Rutten O2 Trainer.

At breakfast, I took a half dozen or more supplements—pills—and drank 16 ounces of freshly pressed green juice, initially a blend of kale and celery, which evolved to just celery. It was the first time each day I looked at my phone. I tried to limit scrolling to 15 minutes getting caught up on texts, email, sports, and news.

Given all the traditional and non-traditional treatments I was exploring, I likely had an afternoon appointment. If not, Jing and I walked together or I met a friend for coffee. I read a ton, rarely about my diagnosis. I read Marcus Aurelius' *Meditations* and Seneca's *On the Shortness of Life*. My lunch likely included fresh vegetables, a salad, or a bean dish. I particularly enjoyed peppers with huge dollops of hummus. I also drank 16 ounces of pressed carrot juice along with any supplements.

Late afternoon, if my stomach wasn't full, I downed a decaf tea or coffee. I often picked up a daughter from school, which was a great lead-in to dinner. Eating together was a high priority and a highlight. I got to hear what happened in everyone's world and tried to inject dad humor wherever possible. I also finished all my prescribed medications and any remaining supplements. By the end of the day, I had drunk 90-110 ounces of liquid and taken 10-20 pills.

In the evening, I fed my fish, a thoroughly enjoyable activity. We then watched a show or played a game. Because I had largely stripped added sugar and stimulants from my diet, my energy was surprisingly constant throughout the day. I didn't experience the dips in energy after lunch and around dinner time that plagued me before my diagnosis. Although that was a definite benefit of my drastic lifestyle changes, I began to run out of gas early in the evening. I usually went to bed before everyone else to ensure I could get 10 hours or more of sleep each night.

DEALING WITH—STUFF

As the days wore on, I had been taking Imatinib for a few months.

This chemotherapy drug is the generic version of Gleevec, which had come off patent in February 2016. The generic had been available for seven years.

Given the expense, my insurance company required I receive my medication by mail from a specialty pharmacy, which shipped 30 pills at a time. However, when I attempted to get my third refill, the pharmacy said they weren't allowed to fill my prescription for another 10 days, meaning I would have to go without it for several days. I walked the customer service person through the simple math of the day I started taking the medicine and added 30 again.

While the representative understood the math, he couldn't override the system. Evidently the system can't do basic math. The issue took two weeks and many hours on the phone to resolve with the specialty pharmacy. The situation injected unnecessary stress into my life, wondering if I would run out. It's another example of a broken healthcare system.

I was on hold during one of these calls. I heeded a friend's suggestion and decided to check out Mark Cuban's pharmacy, CostPlusDrugs.com. Lo and behold, I can get my prescription WITHOUT insurance for $99 for 90 days. I knew I was already personally paying $240 per month for the drug, which adds up to significant money until a deductible is met.

I was curious how much my company had to pay for the drug, so I logged onto my insurance portal and was aghast to see they were paying $6,150 a month! To put that in yearly numbers, the drug cost:

- $396 per year with no insurance through Mark Cuban's pharmacy
- $73,800 per year with insurance only available through a specialty pharmacy

Mark Cuban states on his website that his margin is 15%, so any cost above that is excess margin racked up by the specialty pharmacy and the manufacturers.

$73K in profit per year for a generic drug! How is this even allowed?

As a healthcare executive, I'm concerned about the high price to all of us of a broken system. Because I had maxed my out-of-pocket cost, I was paying nothing while my employer ate more than $6,000 a month. As a consumer, I had no incentive to do anything about it. Other than my outrage!

What did I do? I switched my prescription to CostPlusDrugs.com and received my first 90 days of medication, which came with the added benefit of not having to worry about an agonizing refill process every 30 days. Much to my surprise, the bottle and pills were identical to the ones I received from the specialty pharmacy. In other words, it came from the EXACT SAME manufacturer.

It was suddenly clear that the entity pocketing the extra margin was the specialty pharmacy. To add yet another twisted layer, I receive insurance through a large national for-profit insurer. The specialty pharmacy is owned by a different large national for-profit insurer. So, by forcing me to get my medication through this specialty pharmacy, my insurer guarantees that its competitor will get the excess profits.

Unbelievable on so many levels. A drug that has been "generic" – I use the term loosely – for more than seven years still costs an extraordinary amount above the actual cost of production. This is another example of waste in the system that costs all of us dearly.

MORE PEP FROM AROUND THE WORLD

I wondered if the support I felt when I disclosed my diagnosis to the world would continue. In addition to receiving texts, emails, and letters, I was blessed with in-person visitors:

- One of my medical advisors made a special trip to spend the day with me and my family.
- A couple from my past who live in Iceland came to the United States and joined us for a morning.
- A college friend I hadn't seen in more than two decades visited and gave me a shirt his daughter had custom-made bearing the initials PEP.

My fellow human beings continued their outpouring of love. They were helping heal me with their positivity, energy and prayer. How could I not beat this thing?

THE BIGGEST REPORT CARD OF MY LIFE

My local oncologist said at an earlier appointment that we could do our first scan in two or three months. I had an immediate question. "Why wait three months if we can see how it's going in two?" He acknowledged there was no specific science behind two versus three, and we could ultimately decide. As I continued to get blood work showing my liver levels were completely normal, I knew the drug was working. Why not give it more time to work? I wanted to show maximum progress.

I knew that to get attention from a center of excellence for possible surgery, I needed to prove to them that I was different. I was an n of 1!

I was also sensitive to getting more radiation and dye injected into my system if it wasn't needed. Even with the clarification of creatinine versus cystatin C, it felt safer to push out scans at this point rather than pull them in. As part of this decision, we received guidance that we could do a CT scan without dye. That nudged us toward our answer. We anticipated the radiologist would caveat any findings without contrast, but since this was a progress check, the trade-off felt worth it. So we decided to push out the appointment for three months since I began taking Imatinib.

How did I feel? Great. Extremely optimistic. Until I didn't. About a week before the test, I began feeling nervous. What if I'm not making as much progress as I thought? What if they find something else? What if the cancer got worse? God forbid!

What if...what if...what if?

As I tell our daughters, "What ifs are like infinity. They have no end." Even knowing this, it was difficult to push the What ifs out of my mind. I had read about scan anxiety, and it was hard to appreciate whether it would impact me until I was in it. Scan anxiety had definitely set in, and for the week leading up to the test, I didn't sleep great. My worry was exacerbated by pain one night on the right side of my lower back. The next morning, blood and urine samples at urgent care checked out okay, so I went home, and the pain gradually disappeared.

THE TEST—AND RESULTS

As before, the CT scan happened quickly in the morning, and then we were left to wait for an update to our portal. Unfortunately, we spent the day on edge because the portal didn't update until late that night.

The results indicated my liver spots had decreased significantly, with many of them 50% smaller. That was exciting. But what about the five primary spots on my intestines? The report said, "Interval complete resolution of the pelvic soft tissue masses." This seemed positive, but online searches left us unsure. I reached out to my medical advisors, but it was late.

We were in bed when one advisor called back. He confirmed our hope. The CT scan found no trace of the five spots, even the one that had been the size of a small potato! They had disappeared, they had vanished, they were no more! We were elated.

My wife and I lay in bed that night for a long time, crying tears of joy mixed with shock tinged with anxiety wondering if the wonderful results were real.

Did the lack of contrast mean something was missed?

We were happy to take this win, however, and we were eager to meet with our local oncologist in a few days.

Our oncologist confirmed the results. The primary spots were indeed gone. He was a little perplexed because tumors normally all decrease by the same percentage, but in this case the primary tumors had disappeared and the secondary liver tumors, though significantly reduced, were still there. Nevertheless, this was a phenomenal result in just 90 days. In the back of my mind, I needed it – especially if the medicine quit working in another 270 days.

We quickly pressed on what this meant for surgery. Unlike the oncologists at the centers of excellence, he was at least willing to discuss the topic. He said it comes down to the number of spots more than their size, and we really needed to see low single digits to consider surgery.

I don't know if I was excited because he engaged the question or because of the answer he provided. Either way, it felt like hope. Of the 15 spots, many were tiny. If they had shrunk by 50% in 90 days, it felt possible they could disappear during the next scan, especially since the primary spots were gone.

In the biggest report card of my life, I firmly felt I deserved an 'A' and wasn't going to let anyone take that away from me.

BACK TO WORK

I had told the CEO at work that if my first report card was good, I wanted to return to work, so I was eager to get back and see my coworkers. The cancer diagnosis had taken away my ability to work, so I didn't dread restarting. I was enthusiastic. I don't have to do this – I get to! That simple reframing can make all the difference. My eyes were teary when I joined my first executive call and then again when I traveled to our corporate headquarters. I wasn't sure I would ever see these humans again, and it was a blessing to be with them. All the hugs were great.

One of the conditions for me going back to work was the flexibility to attend a week-long meditation retreat. Meditation had been so critical in getting me to this point that I wanted to expand my knowledge and training through an immersive experience.

Most retreats were booked into the next year or located abroad, which felt like a potential derailer of my healthy eating habits. But there was still a conference in Orlando I could attend. I debated waiting, but I'm always biased to act. So why not go now? Moreover, that internal clock was still counting down the days until the drug might stop working.

> ***If this adventure could help me get and stay in the right mindset to heal my body, then it would totally be worth it.***

With this mindset, I set off to Florida alone to completely immerse myself in meditation. Other than a daily text to my wife, I completely ignored my phone and everything outside the retreat. As it turned out, the experience was far more than I bargained for.

CHAPTER 10:

TRYING ANYTHING

The diagnosis made me intent on healing myself, and suddenly I found myself considering any course of action that might help. Before the diagnosis, I looked skeptically at non-traditional practices like acupuncture, reiki healing and meditation. Post-diagnosis, my world was upended.

> ***I couldn't afford to dismiss any approach that might heal me. My first question had always been "Why?" After my diagnosis, I began to wonder, "Why not?"***

With my life at stake, I was ready to try almost anything that seemed to contain a kernel of truth. It was enough that someone had tried "X" crazy thing, and they were now healed.

So many people had recommended meditation to me that after practicing a couple of core meditations every day for nearly six months, I thought the best way to get better at this life-giving habit was a weeklong intensive meditation retreat.

I signed up without any thought of downsides. How could there be any harm in closing my eyes and focusing inward? Before the retreat, I had no idea meditation came with risks. Had I understood those dangers beforehand, I would have thought hard about going.

Therein lies the lesson I hope others will consider, and it applies to any treatment we hope will improve our wellbeing. If we want to try anything new, we should begin by asking:

What does success look like?
What are the risks?
What are the warning signs?

Those questions are guardrails that keep us on the road to recovery.

I entered an intense meditation experience without wrestling with those questions. I wanted to approach the deeper meditation practices I would learn in the best possible mental state, confident they would work unhindered by negative thoughts. Even if the positive outcome I experienced was pure placebo effect, I believed my state of mind could influence physical results in my body.

Bottom line? If you don't personally explore these questions to evaluate alternative approaches to healing, ask a loved one to do it for you, just as I had my wife dig into the dangerous side effects of traditional medicines.

MEDITATION MINDSET

I started meditating because it made sense to me that I should use my brain to help my body heal. I kept up the habit because it made me feel great.

My daily practices were much less complex than the meditation retreat I attended, which came with a philosophy that predisposed me to ignore warning signs and welcome whatever was to come. A few key points of this thinking:

- There is an all-knowing "source" who directly influences our lives. I call that power "God," but others recognize that source by a different name.
- To connect to the source, we must completely lose ourselves (leave who and what we are in the physical world) and focus on pure consciousness.
- We must let go and stay open to whatever happens, embracing

rather than fighting the experience.
- "Manifestation" is the thing we want to happen in our lives (to be healed, become rich, find love, etc.).
- Meditation experiences focus first on losing ourselves and then on what we want to happen.
- At the conclusion of our meditation, we must believe the manifestation has already happened.
- The manifestation must occur in the way we least expect so we know beyond a shadow of a doubt that our connection to the source caused it to happen.

What did I "manifest"? Not surprisingly, that I would be healed! I imagined exactly how I would know I was healed:

- I saw myself sitting at our kitchen island on my iPad.
- I would get pinged that a new test result was available in my medical portal.
- I would open the message and read, "No indication of previous tumors."
- I would tell my wife, and we would hug and cry over the news.
- We would meet with my oncologist, who would confirm the news.
- I would run out of the office, fall on the grass, and praise God.

It's easy to think "If meditation can cure cancer, why isn't everyone doing it?" However, at this point in my journey, I had read so many stories and talked to so many people healed in non-traditional ways that I thought I was getting in early on something big. And let's face it: I desperately wanted to believe meditation would heal me.

This retreat aligned with what I thought possible. I didn't discover until later that other people had experienced the dangers of meditation on retreats almost identical to the one I participated in.

DISCLAIMER:

What follows is a detailed account of my experiences at the retreat

Warning, I lose control of my mind and body

Many readers will find this section simply unbeleivable and or disturbing

If you wish to skip this section, proceed to Chapter 16 on page (103)

CHAPTER 11:
HOPE FOR HEALING

I began the meditation retreat with all the hope in the world. I found myself among like-minded people with varying levels of confidence we could obtain the best of what we wished for. A large percentage of those present were repeat attendees. A few were intellectually curious newcomers. More than 400 of the 2,000 attendees were seeking healing from an ailment.

> ***The retreat was incredibly uplifting—until the experience nearly destroyed me. Even so, it was on the retreat that I first sensed my cancer had been healed.***

The best way to understand the best and worst of what happened is through a day-by-day account.

DAY 1: SUNDAY

I arrived in Orlando on Sunday, November 12th, full of excitement and anticipation. I was warned during my pre-retreat medical consultation that the retreat would be intense, starting between 4am and 6am and ending around 9pm.

The retreat sign-in area was crowded with welcoming people, including a lady from Minnesota. I decided I had time for a run, and given the schedule ahead, I didn't expect to work out much if at all. I finished a brief run in time to get cleaned up for the opening session.

I found a spot next to two strangers, both very nice, and both repeat attendees. The young woman had a medical condition. We were among 200 people on Team Green, meaning we sat together and ate together.

Retreat sessions started with loud music and people dancing near the stage. A party atmosphere. The schedule for the week consisted of three meditations per day, broken up by teaching and guest speakers. My chemotherapy drug made me sleep 10-12 hours a night, and the long evening sessions would make it a challenge to get anywhere near that. Jing had sent me off with quick prep vegetarian meals I could eat in my room and get to bed quickly.

DAY 2: MONDAY

Monday's long meditations, which lasted an hour or two, stretched far beyond my ability to focus. I had completed over 20 hours of coursework because, prior to the retreat, I could rarely meditate for more than five or ten minutes. I was unsurprised yet frustrated.

One of the meditations introduced was called "The Breath," an effort to activate the pineal gland deep in the brain.

Twice before the retreat, I attempted this meditation and failed. In fact, I woke up in the middle of the night feeling like I couldn't get a deep breath. I have occasionally had this sensation since I was young, but it had never been diagnosed. I knew that it rarely happens when I exercise consistently.

The idea behind "The Breath" is to exert pressure on spinal fluid to activate the pineal gland. You start by exhaling completely and slowly inhaling while clenching muscles from your perineum upward through your lower torso, upper torso, and finally your neck. Holding your breath, you clamp your muscles even tighter. As you feel like you're going to pass out, you take a deep breath and repeat the process. As we did this exercise together, dramatic music played in the background as the instructor implored us to give it our all.

Why this? The belief is that the mind is the world's biggest pharmacy, and activating your pineal gland can stimulate mystical experiences and insights. It seems to create a similar effect to taking hallucinogenic mushrooms.

This specific meditation caused me consternation. Doing anything that might cause me to lose sleep was concerning. Learning that The Breath was the primary focus of the retreat made me even more worried I wouldn't get enough sleep. In retrospect, maybe my reaction was an early warning signal, a blinking dashboard light I ignored.

Like most people that day, I didn't succeed at The Breath.

DAY 3: TUESDAY MORNING

The next morning, a speaker acknowledged that we might feel frustrated. He explained that if we stay in that emotional state, we will stay connected to the physical world and be unable to lose ourselves and connect to the source.

It felt like the speaker's words were aimed right at me, and I did the morning meditation with renewed focus and drive.

We did a meditation that morning around the Seven Energy Centers which are said to exist from the base of the spine to the top of the head. Much to my surprise, I started to feel each energy center beat like a little heart.

Oddly, the energy centers representing my intestines and digestion pulsed much louder than the others. Evidently, if I were in balance, the pulsing should be in-sync and the same volume, but that wasn't the case. Given the cancer was in my intestines and liver, this seemed to indicate they were still out of balance.

MORE DAY 3: TUESDAY AFTERNOON AND EVENING:

That afternoon, we undertook our second meditation focused on The Breath. After a few attempts, I was suddenly somewhere else. Like I was traveling on a Star Wars ship. Bumpy, dark, with brief flashes of white light. My arms seemed to flail. This sensation lasted only a few seconds, and then I realized, "I did it! I connected to my pineal gland!" The instant that thought hit me, I was back in the auditorium with the instructor imploring people to do the exercise. I couldn't get the sensation back. I was simultaneously excited at my accomplishment and worried it would trigger a breathing issue that night.

We finished late. I ate a quick dinner and went to bed. Interestingly, I slept well with no breathing issues.

DAY 4: WEDNESDAY

Wednesday was much like the day before, with morning meditation and teaching. I was slowly getting to know amazing members of the Green Team. Several were dealing with cancer. Surprisingly, I met college students who just wanted to learn. I was jealous they were gaining these insights so early in life and wished I had known about this approach sooner.

Part of the morning teaching focused on love, emphasizing the need to love yourself to become whole as well as asking "What would love do?" The underlying focus on love intuitively felt right to me. How could more love in the world be wrong?

Wednesday afternoon, we did yet another meditation on The Breath. I knew I could do it again if I embraced it and let it happen. This time, I quickly activated my pineal gland. I stayed with it and remained in an altered state where I could still hear the music and instructions but mentally I wasn't totally there. I was seated but felt my body move in a circular motion, sped up, and slowed, lasting the length of the meditation.

At that point, I felt my body being healed. I couldn't give a reason for my feeling but it came with a strong conviction. As usual, we ended the meditation lying on the ground. I came out of the altered state but started crying, overwhelmed that I was healed.

The auditorium was packed tight. On my left was a nice woman from another country, and on my right was a large man I hadn't even said hi to.

After the meditation, I looked at them and said, "I think I've been healed." They looked back at me, sharing my surprise and happiness.

When the man asked if I needed a hug, I wrapped my arms around him and wept at the top of my lungs, the loudest and most emotional crying of my life, so loud that everyone in the auditorium could hear me, even above the announcements. The release felt amazing. Complete strangers and new acquaintances embraced me and sat with me. One said the power of my release brought her to tears, and she had to sit.

Eventually, everyone left the auditorium for a late lunch, and I stayed behind in a state of bliss. I recalled my imagery of how I would discover I was healed—with Jing, at home—to suddenly find I'm healed on a meditation retreat, far from home, hugging a stranger and sobbing uncontrollably. This perfectly fits the mantra of "in the way you least expect." I began laughing uncontrollably.

When the last meditation ended that evening, someone laughed so loudly that everyone could hear. Someone else laughed. And a chain reaction cascaded through everyone. Have you ever heard 2,000 people laughing deep from the belly? Not a manufactured sitcom laugh track. I hadn't, and the experience was remarkable. Genuine laughter is indeed contagious.

I remember thinking that everything about this retreat felt right. I was flying high the rest of the evening, and falling asleep was a challenge because I was so damn happy.

CHAPTER 12:

HEALED!

As the next day began, I still believed I was healed. Yet a bit of doubt crept in. How did activating the pineal gland affect me? Did I trigger a psychedelic experience that wasn't real? Was the whole thing just a hallucination?

DAY 5: THURSDAY MORNING

Thursday started with a walking meditation where each participant downloaded instructions to their phone. We began outside at the same time, first standing still with our eyes closed, then walking in a predefined loop, eyes open but still meditating. We finished lying on the ground.

I was extremely skeptical that anyone could meditate while walking, but I aimed to fully embrace the experience. So I said to myself, "Why not?" During the exercise, I grew surprisingly emotional, yet I wasn't in what I considered a meditative state. The movement felt nice, but that was it. Other attendees clearly had breakthroughs. They cried, yelled, and more.

The previous night, I had been too excited to sleep well, so I went back to my room bent on grabbing a quick nap. As I stared at the ceiling, translucent particles began to fall. As the fragments continued, I started to see the edge of my nose. And then my body convulsed. My arms and legs were jolting, and my head thrashed back and forth on my pillow. In the process, I lost my glasses and the name tag hanging around my neck.

Was I worried? Not one bit.

I heard people could have "experiences" and I should embrace whatever came my way as a natural outcome of removing the filter between my conscious and subconscious. As my body shook, I fully believed I was conscious and gaining additional proof of my healing. What happened didn't require The Breath. Or a speaker. Or music. Or a crowd. Just me alone in my hotel room.

***I was ecstatic about it all.
The convulsions grew so strong
I eventually fell off the bed
before they subsided.***

I landed in an odd position with my right hand and right foot both near the base of the bed. I lay still until both body parts began rhythmically tapping the base of the wooden bed. My body convulsed again. Keeping with the mantra of "embrace it," I let it happen.

When the convulsions halted, the first thing that popped into my head was, "I love me." The talk the day before forced me to face a few facts. First, I think I'm a pretty good guy. Second, I try to do the right thing. Third, I don't really love myself. I have a terrible habit of expending all my energy on outside endeavors—primarily work—and leaving nothing for myself to recover. I wouldn't do that if I really loved myself!

I begin chanting "I love me." I continued the chant with different intonations, speeding up until the words became indecipherable.

My body again began convulsing. My cell phone dropped from my pocket onto the floor.

***At that point, I fully believed I
was healed and directly
connected to the source.***

Down on the floor, other deep thoughts came to mind. A month before the retreat, I had a crazy idea for a healthcare company I could start. The concept was so audacious I repeatedly dismissed it. But the thought kept returning. I had also come to realize that my life's happiness didn't depend on achieving my lifelong goal of becoming a CEO. While I enjoyed serving as CEO at Landmark Health, an in-home healthcare company, that stint didn't feel like it counted. To make my idea happen, however, I would need to found an organization and likely take the lead as CEO.

Pondering this big idea, the words "Souls to Heal" filled my mind. I believed my idea was so enormous that I would need the best and brightest to join me ("souls") to heal America's broken healthcare system. Just like before, I repeated the phrase with different intonations, speeding up until I again began convulsing.

Again my body quieted. Next, my mom popped into my head 15 months after her passing. I talked to her, believing she could hear me. I repeatedly said how much I loved her and missed her. I then verbalized what I thought she was saying to me.

Mom always called me Christopher when she was fake-mad at me, so we began a dialogue with me speaking both sides:

- "Christopher, what are you doing here?"
- "Surprised you, didn't I?"
- "Christopher, how did you get here?"
- "Didn't think I could do it, did you?"

I repeated this conversation a few times and raised my arms as if giving my mom a virtual hug. I moved my arms back and forth, cradling her and saying I love you.

The motion caused my body to convulse yet again. At that point, my head and heart felt overwhelmed with goodness. I was thinking:

- I'm healed.
- I now know I love myself.
- I've found my next professional calling.
- I got more closure with my mom.
- What else could possibly be going on?

My convulsions became more violent. Eventually my chest was forced off the ground, and I erupted in a horrible sound, the deepest guttural cry a human can make. I shrieked until I was completely out of breath and fell back to the ground. I caught my breath and again was thrust upward. This went on for several minutes.

I still wasn't worried. I accepted everything as another sign of the cancer exiting my body.

Then it stopped. That had to be it, right?

I was on the floor looking upward, and the walls began moving in impossible ways, folding onto themselves. When the movement paused, I decided the experience was done and got up.

I saw physical evidence that I hadn't been hallucinating. My glasses and nametag were strewn on the bed, and my phone lay on the floor. It all seemed fitting. Losing my nametag in the convulsions confirmed I was a nobody. Losing my phone meant I was nowhere, lacking a connection to the material world.

I had been in this altered state for over an hour. I felt like I could have halted the convulsions at any time, yet I embraced them and let my mind and body go where they wanted.

MORE DAY 5: THURSDAY AFTERNOON

I was in near euphoria after the morning experience and relayed it to a few people at lunch. They were amazed. I didn't realize how rare my experience was.

The final meditation of the day was the first coherence healing, where 200 "healees" were selected to be healed by the remaining 1,800 "healers." The healees entered the auditorium in advance, each lying on the ground on a blanket with four chairs on the left and four on the right. I put my pillow, blanket, and eye covering in place; nothing else was allowed except my room key and healee badge. I closed my eyes and began a deep breathing exercise. I was exceptionally nervous, having no idea what to expect. We were given simple instructions to "open ourselves up to love."

When the healers entered, the room felt electric, like energy surging through the air all around me. Even before my eight healers reached me, my body began convulsing. I embraced it and let my arms and legs move. I could feel my healers approach. As they sat and closed their eyes, my lower torso thrust up and down. I repeatedly hit the ground with such force I worried I would be sore, but I didn't stop it. I assumed my body was just trying to create the biggest wave of energy it could for my healing. After all, another mantra of the teaching was "Be the wave."

Once the meditation commenced, my chest pushed up off the ground and I again spewed that horrible guttural sound at the top of my lungs until I was out of breath. We were surrounded by all sorts of noises, from screaming to crying to other bizarre sounds. It was a weird, energy-filled cacophony, but I attempted to focus on myself.

I continued making my terrible noise for the entire session. As the meditation ended, I lay there unsure if I was ready to remove my mask. When I did, eight faces stared back at me. It was intensely emotional. I cried my thanks for helping me, and each hugged me. One lady said, "It sounded like Satan was coming out of your mouth."

I slowly collected my things and headed back to my room for dinner. I ate quickly, feeling so alive because I had just gotten rid of more of the cancer in my body, or so I thought. I walked around the massive hotel facility, an enclosed structure with what looks like an old Spanish fortress in the center.

Every night I got less and less sleep. I decided I needed to try to rest before Friday's morning meditation.

CHAPTER 13:
MORE HEALING SIGNS

I still view my first six days of the meditation retreat as helpful. Events, although often unexpected and sometimes strange, gave me no signs or feelings I interpreted as negative. Even as my body shook and my mouth projected the worst sounds imaginable, I was certain my body was expelling bad stuff.

I believe more than ever in the power of the mind, and on the retreat my mind took in positive experiences that I still can't interpret in a negative light. I was in a deep spiritual process that restored me in mind, body and soul. It was the first time in my life I loved myself. Everything I experienced validated my reasons for attending.

What happened late Friday night was decidedly different. There were no warm thoughts or feelings. There was only terror.

Before that turning point, however, there were several more unexpected signs of my healing.

DAY 6: FRIDAY 3:15 AM

My alarm woke me to prepare for the grand finale of the week, the

Pineal Gland meditation. Retreat leaders made clear we had to be in the auditorium by 4am or we wouldn't be allowed to participate. Most people had yet to activate their pineal gland, and all our practice pointed to this moment. In this last push to stimulate the pineal gland, there were promises of mystical experiences.

I didn't care about that. I didn't need a mystical road trip. I came to get healed. But there was so much buildup to this session I had to go. I arrived outside the auditorium around 3:30 AM and was surprised to see a winding line to get in. I found a chair next to two guys I had met.

We would do The Breath multiple times that morning, combined with another technique of rapidly inhaling and exhaling, repeated multiple times.

I quickly activated my pineal gland and again transitioned to a different state. I didn't gain any deep insights but I enjoyed the experience. When we moved to a phase lying on the ground, I left the altered state. When we retook our seats, I couldn't do it again. I was cold. I wrapped myself not only in blankets but in towels I brought for cushioning. I was so damn freezing in a meat locker of an auditorium for over four hours that I just wasn't trying hard and wanted it to be over with.

As we prepared for a second coherence healing, we were just as charged with anticipation and excitement as the first.

I repeated everything as before—blanket, pillow, eye mask. I sensed the energy when the healers entered the auditorium, but my body lay motionless except for minor twitches. Once I felt my healers approach, my body moved forcefully. My arms swung down from above my head to slap the ground near my hips. Again and again, they flew up and came slamming down hard.

The forceful slapping continued as my healers took their seats and were instructed to shut their eyes. At one point, someone grabbed my ankles and my left arm. The energy instantly left my body, and I went limp. "What a bummer" was my immediate thought. I was out of energy to help heal myself, but maybe I no longer needed it because I was already healed.

I was surprised someone halted my movement. Healers and staff weren't to intervene with healees unless they were hurting themselves. What I was doing was far less violent than what my back and butt suffered the day before.

As the meditation progressed, energy returned to my body, and my chest was again thrown off the ground, with the same nasty sounds emanating from my body's depths. This cycle repeated multiple times. Until it suddenly stopped.

I started crying profusely, believing the nastiness was at last completely out of my system.

After crying for a bit, my chest was thrown up one last time. But this instance was different. Rather than projecting a nasty sound forward, it was as if the sound was scraped from my mouth, stripped out completely, and left above my head. After this, all the energy was out of my body, and shortly after, the meditation ended.

I removed my eye mask and looked into the eyes of eight healers with relief and utter gratitude. We all hugged and thanked each other.

A woman on my far left asked why I stopped slapping the ground so hard. I said it was because two people grabbed me. This experienced meditator said the energy in the room was unbelievably high that night, so high that spirits could interact with humans. While she could feel the spirits, they never allowed her to see them. Looking around during meditation is forbidden, but when I stopped slapping, she opened her eyes. No one was touching me. This woman believed the spirits were present to help me. While I didn't really know what to think, it seemed like more good news for me.

Also on my left was a mother and daughter, who was the same age as our older daughter, 17. The mother told me during the meditation that she became very large. Bigger than the world. Bigger than the solar system. She floated directly above me, pulling what looked like black smoke rings out of my body one after another. She kept doing this until she got the message that it was done. She told me, "I don't know what you have, but whatever it is—it's gone." Yet another crazy story helping to confirm I'm healed.

As everyone began to leave, a third woman on my left side came up to me privately said she too had opened her eyes. "It was when you stopped making noise. There was no one around you." I took this as even more proof that higher powers were helping me heal.

If I was flying high the night before, I was experiencing pure bliss that night. I ate quickly in my room and enjoyed my last night at the conference venue. I walked slowly around its immense interior, listening to Christian music and crying quietly as I tried to soak up as much of this amazing venue as possible.

I was so excited to go home and tell my wife and kids everything that happened to me—and share the news that I was healed from my stage 4 cancer!

Eventually, I decided to go back to my room. I needed a decent night of sleep before the last day of the retreat. A few hours later, early Saturday morning, everything fell apart.

CHAPTER 14:

TO HELL AND BACK

DAY 7: SATURDAY 2:00 AM

I awoke at 2am feeling amazingly rested. The clock said I had another three hours before I had to get up. Excited that I already felt good and anticipated doing even better with more sleep, I rolled back over.

I couldn't settle back. My feet felt like they were on fire with energy. They slowly started moving, and I threw off the covers, embracing the mantra of "let it happen," yet unsure what my body needed to do. I convulsed to the point that I fell out of bed, square between the two queen beds, my head toward the bottom and my arms and legs at my sides. I felt like a pencil.

At some point, I took off my underwear. Every muscle in my naked body began to clench with unbelievable rigidity. I grew so tense I urinated all over myself. I thought, *Is this necessary? Why do I need to be naked? Why am I urinating? How am I going to clean this up?*

My body contorted uncomfortably. I was forcing up on my heels while attempting to bend my neck back so my forehead could touch the ground, a physical impossibility for a middle-aged man. Noise continually emerged from my mouth, much softer and less guttural than before.

When I tried to shift my legs, I felt extreme pain as I was forced back to a pencil position. My body clearly wanted me to do something, but

I had no idea what. With extreme pressure building in my forehead, I became scared as my body kept wrenching against itself. As time wore on, I managed to flip from my back and press my forehead and pelvis hard into the ground, desperate to relieve the head pressure.

Maybe I needed to poop. I forced my body to the toilet. I didn't need to go, but the pressure in my head was so intense I pressed it on the cold bathroom floor.

When I finally regained control of my body, I checked the clock. More than three hours had passed.

I was terrified. I no longer believed I could control my body's movements.

DAY 7: SATURDAY 5:30 AM

I cleaned up in the shower, then posted a panicked message in the one retreat group chat available. I gave my name, room number, and cell, and stated that I was scared I was losing control of my body and mind.

No response.

I sat outside my hotel room door. Everyone was getting ready for the final morning of the retreat. Multiple people asked if I was okay. I wasn't. Someone got me to the retreat Help Desk. I immediately began balling to the first person I met.

As I sat on the floor sipping water, the retreat's lead emotional support person asked how she could help. I relayed what happened that night, as well as the entirety of the retreat and my cancer diagnosis. Her explanation during one of these "events" that it was totally natural to pee—or poop or puke—didn't comfort me. If it happened again, I should just let it!

This advice only amplified my terror. I was due on a plane later that afternoon to see my wife and kids. I didn't want them to see any of what just happened. It would scare them to death.

I told the designated emotional support person more of my life story, including my upbringing and professional success. She replied that I was one of a handful at the conference with such power of meditation. It was a "gift". I reiterated my mortification at urinating. I felt horrible about the mess I caused. She told me the episode was a battle between my mind and soul. My soul wanted to demonstrate that it was the absolute boss over my mind. My mind wants control, but the soul has real control of everything.

She repeated that I shouldn't be alarmed if it happens again.

She said she had to leave.

I didn't want to do any more meditation. I was now terrified of something I had eagerly embraced just a day earlier. Her parting words were that I should stay near "the flock" but not directly participate.

DAY 7: SATURDAY 7:00 AM

From this point forward, I had the mind of a child. I had no critical filter, and whatever anyone said went right into my brain.

We did a walking meditation that final morning. I picked a favorite tree to ground my body on and spent the meditation hugging this tree. I felt my body pulsing with energy. I knew I had drawn way too much of it, not sure how, but I did. I begged the tree to take the energy from me. I pressed my forehead into the trunk, trying to force the energy out of me.

At breakfast, I chose to sit by myself, still pulsing, to avoid conversations. I nevertheless decided to join the big group for the last instructional session in the auditorium. My stomach started to hurt, and I felt like I needed to poop. My mind raced. How could I finish this "final battle" of mind and soul before I went home? I couldn't let this epic clash spill over in front of my family. If I could help it at all, I wouldn't let it happen in front of my wife or, worse, my kids. I decided to get it over with by letting my spirit prove its dominance over my mind. Hopefully, I could put a bow on it and leave. I still clung to the belief that events needed to unfold in a way I least expected to know my healing was true.

I headed to the nearest restroom, a space built for a crowd. Faced with multiple rows of urinals and stalls, I shut myself in the stall furthest from the entrance and proceeded to remove all my clothes. I urinated on myself the last time I went crazy, and I anticipated this would be worse. After pooping, still on the toilet, I felt intense stomach pain, like a haymaker straight to the midsection.

I gagged, sputtered, and spat. At the moment, I believed I threw up. Out of ideas on how to end the battle, I began to chant, "I surrender." I repeated the words louder and louder to the point of yelling. I felt my eyes roll back into my head. As my yelling slurred, I threw my naked body to the bathroom floor, hoping the conflict would end.

My body started convulsing, and I realized the battle was still raging. I wondered what else I needed to do. When I urinated on myself again, I was like, "Who cares! At least it's not carpet." With my body still convulsing, I gripped the toilet seat, hung my head above the bowl, and flushed. I screamed.

"I surrender!" And I put my head into the toilet water. I thought that would be enough. This was happening in a way I least expected.

It wasn't enough. I was still convulsing. I put my head into the toilet again, deep enough for toilet water to fill my nostrils. I came up for air and expelled the water as forcefully as I could. I threw myself on the ground and waited. I said to myself, "That has to be fucking enough. We are done".

My body quieted. I realized it was finally over. I was naked and needed help.

I exited the stall naked and fell into a child's pose, on my knees, face to the floor, arms outstretched in front of me. "Help me."

Eventually several people showed up, including the retreat's emotional support leader. They shut down the entire restroom, and multiple people helped me put my clothes back on. I asked for a shower.

They led me to a conference room where a mix of hotel staff, retreat personnel, and EMTs descended on me. They tested my blood sugar. It was fine. I was full of water and Gatorade. I felt fine. Most of all, I was relieved the war between my body and spirit was over. When I explained that to the emotional support leader, she had none of it. She said I went too far when I put my head in the toilet.

What happened to "It had to happen in the way I least expected"?

She accused me of playing games. It was a very tense conversation. So much for emotional support. A physician assistant (PA) stated I should go to the hospital and get checked out, adding that everyone from the hotel staff to EMTs recommended it. She also asked for my permission to call my wife to let her know what happened. I agreed.

***I was loaded into an ambulance.
As I spoke to Jing, she sobbed
uncontrollably and asked me
what happened. What is going on?***

I attempted to reassure Jing that I was fine and that the hospital ride was just a precaution. I spoke long enough to our younger daughter to tell her I had been healed from my cancer and couldn't wait to see them and tell them all about it. Jing informed me she was flying down to get me, and we would fly back together.

I felt horrible that I made my family so upset.

CHAPTER 15:
AT THE HOSPITAL

DAY 7: SATURDAY 3:00 PM

After I was unloaded from the ambulance and wheeled on a gurney into the hospital, I let the intake team do their tasks. When the emergency room doctor stepped into my bay, I asked why I was there.

"We think the cancer has spread to your brain," he said. "We need to do a CT scan."

"No fucking way it's spread," I replied.

I attempted to explain to the doctor what had transpired during the week. He ran down his diagnostic checklist. Did I drink any tea? Did I take any drugs? Had I experienced any of these unusual symptoms before? To each item, I stated an emphatic no.

I was unaware that the meditation retreat provider had spoken with the hospital and already called my wife and told her I had a psychotic episode and its suspected origin.

As I talked with Jing, I didn't know she feared the cancer had invaded my brain. I still can't believe the meditation provider gave my wife a horrifying, unverified diagnosis without informing me. How incredibly reckless.

Within minutes of getting a call from Jing, our dear friends in Tampa were responding. Blake was driving to Orlando to see me. He arrived in time for my CT. Unsurprising to me, the scan was negative. I proceeded to pour out to Blake everything that happened to me, and he assured Jing that I was fine.

When the ER doctor couldn't find anything wrong with me, I was discharged. Blake and I went back to the conference hotel and grabbed dinner as I anxiously awaited Jing's arrival. In that moment, I was totally convinced everything I had described so far was real—that it happened exactly as I perceived it.

I'm now far less sure. I should have been filthy from everything I did, yet people saw no need to help me clean up before slipping me back into my clothes. I now believe I was conscious until my eyes rolled in the back of my head, and everything from that point forward indeed happened inside my brain. When I texted the meditation provider asking her if I was dirty, she never responded. The distancing had begun.

DAY 7: SATURDAY 10:00 PM

Blake and I were sitting inside the hotel entrance when I saw my wife walking in. I rushed to meet her. She broke down as we embraced. Her sobbing made me feel even more horrible about the pain I was causing. When Blake left, Jing and I booked a new room at the hotel. In hindsight, I wish we had stayed somewhere, anywhere else. We planned to stay the night and fly home the next day.

I told my wife everything that happened. She looked me in the eye and said my behavior in the bathroom wasn't normal. Did I agree? I did. Jing had difficulty reconciling all the amazing things I experienced during the first six days of the retreat with the trauma of the last 24 hours. Me? I was still relieved my mind/spirit battle was over and grateful I was healed.

Showering before bed, I still didn't feel quite right. My body still pulsated with some level of energy. I lay down and shut my eyes, but images flitted across my mind so fast I couldn't even discern what they were. The thought of sleeping made me paranoid. I tried to force my mind to think of a happy movie scene but failed. The racing images wouldn't stop.

My wife said we couldn't go home unless I got some sleep, and I fully agreed. I was desperate to go home but terrified of closing my eyes. Jing and I had the same discussion multiple times. At one point, she said I had been sleeping for an hour and a half and needed more before we could go home. I instantly rejected the idea that I had been sleeping. I argued that we just had this conversation five minutes ago, and five minutes before that, and five minutes before that.

I felt terrified. I wondered if I was stuck in meditation or drifting in an alternate reality. I began questioning if Jing was actually there. I worried I was losing my mind, which to me was even more chilling than a cancer diagnosis.

Unable to trust my own thoughts or the words of my wife, I said I needed to go back to the hospital so they could figure out what was wrong with me.

My wife reminded me that if we went to the hospital we couldn't go home. I understood. She cried as we decided that getting help was indeed necessary.

Jing has never seen me like this. She wanted to call an Uber, but I demanded an ambulance. I didn't trust Uber to get us there quickly, and I felt like I could lose control at any moment. Jing acquiesced and called 911. It took so long for the ambulance to show up that I thought she hadn't called. I peppered Jing with questions about when she arrived, how we met, and other facts from our past. I was trying to confirm she was real.

The ambulance still wasn't there, so I decided we should wait outside at the entrance. I went out and grabbed a tree in a large pot, again attempting to ground myself and release the energy in my body. When the ambulance finally arrived, the EMTs who loaded me up wouldn't let Jing ride in back with me, which only caused me to further suspect she wasn't real.

DAY 8: SUNDAY MORNING

My body felt like it could begin convulsing at any moment, and I focused hard on holding it at bay. Once at the hospital, I was given Ativan so I could rest. Blake and Beth drove from Tampa back to Orlando, and we all spent the afternoon in a hospital that looked like a Four Seasons hotel.

The emergency room doctor was adamant about doing an MRI of my brain. I argued that I was already dosed with radiation from a CT scan, which came back negative. If an MRI was necessary, they should have done that first. Obviously, the doctor and I didn't get along. They gave me an IV but refused to discharge me until I signed a document that I was going against medical direction. They also refused to give me even a single Ativan post-discharge so I could sleep that night. They clearly thought I was drug-seeking; I thought they were beyond ridiculous.

We decided to leave Orlando behind and spend the night at our friends' house in Tampa. For the first time in days, I felt like myself, which came as a great relief. The car ride was enjoyable; we had a nice dinner out and got to see their place for the first time. Snug in their guest bedroom, I went to sleep with no problems.

Something changed a few hours later. I woke up and felt my entire body pulsing. It was the strongest sensation I ever felt.

My wife and Blake assured me that everything was fine and that I just needed to go back to sleep. My wife had never seen my convulsions and I realized I was exerting immense effort to hold them back. I feared that if I let the energy take me, I might not make it. I might die! I looked my wife directly in the eyes and in the event this was the end, I told her where I stored my letters to our daughters, again causing her immeasurable pain. Jing and Blake finally convinced me to relax and go to sleep.

DAY 8: SUNDAY MIDDLE OF THE NIGHT

After a short sleep, my body awakened full of energy. My legs and arms slammed to my sides in a pencil formation. I began slapping my legs together so hard that Jing was terrified I would break the bones in my feet. My arms moved as well. I could hear Jing and Blake talking, but I wasn't completely there.

Just like before, my chest thrust upward, and once again I made that horrible sound, a cycle that repeated over and over. I felt an unbelievable pressure in my forehead and started chanting "MRI." With my body convulsing, I demanded to go to the ER. By that point, I believed cancer might indeed be in my brain. That would at least explain my convulsions.

I again refused to take an Uber and pleaded for an ambulance. My convulsions stopped as soon as the ambulance pulled up. For the third night in a row, I was in an ambulance on my way to the hospital. What was happening to me?

With some difficulty, the EMTs placed me on a gurney and into the ambulance. I was extremely cold and was rude to the EMT who wouldn't let my wife ride with me. I guess it isn't like the movies. Jing later said the event was the most terrifying thing she had seen in her life. Blake said I looked like I was possessed by the devil and needed an exorcism.

DAY 9: MONDAY EARLY MORNING

The Tampa hospital agreed to do the MRI and a full neurological work-up. They also give me an Ativan to calm me. For the first time in days, I slept for an extended period. This hospital was nothing like the Four Seasons. I was alone in a dingy shared room big enough for three patients. Jing initially wanted me transferred anywhere else, but everyone was so nice we decided to stay.

My wife and I talked and cried. I didn't know what was happening to me, how to fix it, or if I would ever get my mind back. Jing and my dad began working on arranging medical transport so I could fly home and seek admission to a hospital or psychiatric ward there. Inpatient psych units aren't nice places, but I would happily sign myself in so my daughters wouldn't see me like this.

I never thought in a million years
I would voluntarily enter an
inpatient psych ward, but I was
almost happy at the prospect.
I didn't know what else to do.

CHAPTER 16:
THE DAM BURSTS

DAY 9: MONDAY LATE MORNING

Unlike the Orlando hospital, which seemingly just wanted to conduct expensive tests on commercially insured patients, the Tampa hospital sent a psychologist to meet me. I was cautious. Why did I need a shrink?

Jing sat in on the conversation. The psychologist started by asking me about everything that happened at the retreat. Then he inquired how I was doing with the cancer diagnosis. "It must suck," he remarked, sounding like he meant it. I recounted key events since my diagnosis without a word about how I felt.

As far as I was concerned, I was simply sticking to the facts. When Jing mentioned I recently lost my mom to Stage 4 lung cancer, I added details about mom's rapid decline and the drama around her funeral. Listening intently, Jing asked why I didn't tell the psychologist that my dad left me out of the meeting with the pastor. "Yeah, you're right," I replied. "I was fucking furious." Why didn't I tell him about that? For context, my dad and sister met with the pastor before the funeral—a meeting I wasn't included in and only discovered later.

After a while, the psychologist said he expected the MRI and neurological workup to come back clear. I wholeheartedly agreed. Then he ventured into unexpected territory, prefacing his remarks with a statement that "I normally don't go this far with patients on their first visit, but—"

> ***The psychologist said I wasn't owning my feelings. He assured me it was okay to be sad, mad, or pissed. He suggested I was burying my feelings deep inside and suppressing specific memories.***

With this revelation, the dam burst wide open. I sobbed. I declared how badly I wanted to live. I longed to see my daughters graduate from high school and college and walk them down the aisle. The possibility I might not do any of those things made me incredibly sad.

As I talked, the pressure I felt in my forehead suddenly vanished. I sensed the energy drip slowly out of my forehead and leave my body. The psychologist's skill in diagnosing my suffering and pushing me to address my underlying issues—in one visit—was mind-blowing. He saved my life. I likely would have been in a psych ward without him. I will forever think of him as my Angel in Tampa.

DAY 9: MONDAY NIGHT

Jing desperately needed rest after everything I put her through. I urged her to leave and sleep at our friends' place. I took an Ativan and slept for several hours without issues. I got a roommate who wasn't so fortunate. I heard all about his medical history. He didn't eat, downed a daily 12-pack of beer, needed a motorized device to move from his couch to the bathroom, and hadn't pooped in more than a week. He had what sounded like nasty bedsores. He was clearly suffering from alcohol withdrawal. I felt bad for him. I also wasn't sure how HIPAA (Health Insurance Portability and Accountability Act), which protects patients' health information, applied in a shared room.

DAY 10: TUESDAY MORNING

Jing was finalizing details for medical transport when the Tampa hospital discharged me. Medical transport, however, only worked for direct transfers from one hospital to another. A commercial flight was now our only way home. Jing asked if I thought I could fly commercial. Was I worried I might have an episode? I responded that airports and planes are among the world's most comfortable places for me. For three decades, I have flown frequently for work. She booked a flight for later that day. The hospital wouldn't give me any Ativan for the trip, so I "took" one right before I left, which conveniently ended up in Jing's purse.

I watched a movie on the flight home, not nervous at all. My dad picked us up at the airport and immediately wanted to know what happened. I wasn't ready to talk about it, which caused ongoing tension between us. I was so happy to see my girls and give them the biggest bear hugs possible.

I took the Ativan but didn't sleep well. I was worried I would have a convulsion and scare my girls.

DAY 11: WEDNESDAY (THE DAY BEFORE THANKSGIVING)

I was lucky to see my primary care doctor right away, but I was a shell of my former self, no longer the high-flying healthcare executive. I was disheveled and exhausted. I broke down in her office and sobbed about how sad I was. She stepped in with the same great care and comfort she has provided since my diagnosis. She finished by prescribing Lexapro and Klonopin. I didn't realize Klonopin is a seizure med, but it allowed me to sleep without fear.

THE POWER OF WESTERN PSYCHIATRIC MEDICINE

Lexapro and Klonopin pills are only slightly bigger than pinheads, but they pack an amazing punch. The first night I took Klonopin, it was like my brain had been unplugged. Nothing there but complete blackness.

I marveled at how these tiny pills got me through the night. It was clear I needed them to recover from my brain's dysregulated state. It also reinforced the fragility of the human brain. I remembered how low sodium levels plunged my mom into incoherence. The lack of one everyday substance caused her to lose her mind!

Just like I needed Gleevec to help my body overcome cancer, I absolutely needed these pills to help my mind recover.

Without the help of the psychologist and these mental health medications, I'm certain I would be insane or dead.

When I got home, I began taking the full dose of Lexapro, which made me so tired I needed a nap, and when I woke up, I felt more than a little weird. I again started to wonder if anything was real. Ironically, the anti-anxiety medication caused me considerable anxiety. We sent our girls to sleep at my dad's so I didn't worry about them at night.

DAY 12: THANKSGIVING

I got great news that one of my best friends from Chicago was driving up for Thanksgiving, skipping his family celebration to be with us. I told him everything that happened to me—the good, the bad, and the ugly. Interestingly, as I poured out the story, the spot between my eyes again started dripping with energy. Telling the story seemed to help me heal and release pent-up energy. My friend ended up staying with us for almost a week before I was ready for our girls to come home at night. I'm forever grateful for the gift of those days together.

CHAPTER 17:

THE DAYS BEYOND

I clearly needed help processing everything that had just happened to me. I begin "dating" therapists to find the right one. Too bad it's a lot harder than swiping left or right to get a therapist appointment! I tried counselors in person, virtual, peer-to-peer, and faith-based. I said up front that I needed them to push me because my mind was incredibly obstinate.

I wasn't sure if I could open up again like I did in Florida, even knowing full transparency was essential to my healing.

Combined with my other appointments, I had difficulty "dating" so many therapists at once. After several exploratory sessions, I decided the in-person counselor recommended by my oncologist was the best fit.

The week after Thanksgiving, Timothy Ferriss released his weekly podcast, "The Hidden Risk of Meditation".[1]

The hair stood up on the back of my neck and sent shivers through my body. He released this podcast literally days after my psychotic episode, yet another synchronicity event since my diagnosis. Who else went through what I did? Who knew closing your eyes and focusing inward could be dangerous?

I knew I wasn't ready to listen to the podcast, so Jing listened instead. Paraphrasing her: Tim Ferriss was at a weeklong retreat where he "broke." Fortunately, a master was present to help him process his experience. Clearly, there was no master in Florida to help me as I spun out of control. Ferris' interviewee, Dr. Willoughby Britton, is a licensed clinical psychologist, Director of Brown University's Clinical and Affective Neuroscience Laboratory and founder of the Cheetah House, a non-profit that helps meditators in distress.

Ferris and Britton discussed the type of individuals most at risk of a bad meditation experience. It wasn't the sickest, the oldest, or the least experienced. The people most likely to go off the rails are CEOs and other high achievers accustomed to pushing through anything to achieve a goal.

After listening to the podcast, Jing agreed. "They described you perfectly," she said. "You fit the prime profile for a bad meditation experience." I wasn't surprised. No matter how tired I was at the retreat, I went to every single meditation, plus all the other sessions. I embraced the challenge. Getting up at 3:15 AM? No problem.

I immediately made an appointment with a peer counselor at Cheetah House. In my first appointment, I explained everything I went through during my retreat. He said I wasn't alone, and unfortunately, many people have this type of reaction to intensive meditation retreats.

My peer counselor compared meditation to a drug. You can overdose. You need the proper training to take bigger amounts. On one level, that shocked me. Prior to my own experience, I had never heard of anyone having a bad meditation experience. The idea of overdosing sounded crazy. On another level, it made complete sense to me.

While I had meditated diligently for at least an hour every day for months before the retreat, I rarely attempted the meditations we did that week. I wanted so badly to be healed that I outdid others with my focus. My intensity, combined with the lack of a master guide, meant I jumped into the deep end of the pool determined to hold my breath to reach the bottom. Unsurprisingly, I nearly drowned myself trying. I almost killed myself in the process.

Because my peer counselor had also had very good and very bad meditation experiences, he was perfectly suited to help me process all my baggage.

UNPACKING MY BAGGAGE

In the weeks after Thanksgiving, I spoke with many people about what happened in Florida. Each discussion was helpful in its own way and imparted useful insights.

I kept coming back to one question: Could I have broken through my emotional blockages without my near-death experience in Florida?

I would love to think I could have talked with a psychologist for a few months and made steady progress, owning my emotions and understanding how my mind was editing bad memories and experiences. But I'm highly skeptical that process alone would have revealed everything my mind had suppressed for decades.

I believe I had to be completely broken for real emotional healing to begin. In my mind, I pictured putting lock upon lock upon lock on that part of my subconscious, and nothing short of a seismic blast could break those locks and blow the doors wide open to what was hidden. Obviously, I will remain forever thankful for my Angel in Tampa for starting the rescue operation that saved me.

My views of everything that happened in Florida continue to change. First, it was immediately clear that my wife had been to hell and back. My every thought of Florida causes me pain and sorrow as I realize how much agony I put her through. We have discussed these events multiple times. She doesn't blame me. But I do.

Second, it became clear I will need a long time to fully process my experiences. The positivity of the first six days was so high and the negativity of a near-death experience in the final days and weeks that followed was so low. How should I think about that in totality?

I have continued to speak with my talk therapist, acupuncturist, friends, and peer counselors. I have dialogued with people steeped in the Christian faith as well as an assistant professor at Brown University specializing in psychosomatic recovery from meditation. These new realizations have emerged:

- Just because it's possible for leaders to create environments that elicit such positive emotions doesn't mean they should. Even if these environments exist, it doesn't mean you should expose yourself to them.

- Anything that can create intensely positive experiences can also create the same amplitude of negative outcomes. Meditation groups need ample emotional and spiritual support available to humans who end up on the negative side.

- As humans, we are sentient. We have agency. Any surrender of our ability and freedom to think independently and critically is among the worst injuries we can inflict on ourselves and the deepest betrayals of our humanity. I'm ashamed to admit I was so stupid, so naïve, and so unsuspecting.

- I'm committed to speaking up about these issues for the sake of my own mental and physical health as well as the well-being of others.

Why bring up this unflattering part of my story? Because our well-intentioned attempts to find healing can kill us.

Madison Marriage of the Financial Times spent more than a year researching people who suffered bad effects from meditation retreats. In a couple of instances, individuals died by suicide after retreats much like the one I attended. Many others never recovered mentally. Decades later, they still suffer.

Jing listened to Marriage's four-part podcast twice over two days.[2] My wife was rightfully raging mad at the organization that sponsored the meditation retreat.

I feel more guilty than ever that I willingly signed up and paid significant money to nearly die and in the process cause so much pain to the people I love the most. I now realize:

- It's a miracle I'm alive
- It's a miracle I've largely recovered physically and mentally
- While my wife's journey was different, we have both been to hell and back.

One final caution: Any retreat that makes you meditate most of the day should set off alarm bells. Unless you are very experienced, there's too much risk for the potential rewards.

If you are considering attending a meditation retreat, please ensure you have the proper training and that the retreat leaders have the proper support in place.

END NOTES

1 **Tim Ferriss.** *Dr. Willoughby Britton on Meditation, Trauma, and Adverse Effects.* Blog interview, 2023. https://tim.blog/2023/11/22/dr-willoughby-britton/

2 **Financial Times.** *Untold: The Retreat — An Investigative Podcast on the Risks and Harms of Meditation Retreats.* Podcast series, 2022. https://www.ft.com/content/b3ec8e57-5cf9-4f96-9267-56c3bcd9c102

CHAPTER 18:

SELF-DISCOVERY AND REMISSION

As the days passed in December, several realizations jumped out at me. I slowly returned to my routine of exercising, acupuncture, and part-time work. But I didn't go back to any kind of meditation. I wasn't ready for even seemingly benign sessions.

Interestingly, after going for a run, I often laid still, sensing I could instantly drop into a meditative state. It made me feel uneasy. I didn't know what would happen if I went over the edge, and I didn't trust I could control it. So I backed away from the precipice by making myself sit up and stretch.

As I've learned more about our conscious and subconscious minds and the deep interconnections between our mind, body, and spirit, I've noticed how events of the day often creep back at night, bringing important lessons I otherwise might not have heard.

I now recognize that if I don't properly acknowledge and deal with the emotions I experience during the day, I'll feel their lingering effects that night.

If I don't go through my nightly mental routine and clear those emotions, for example, my body might twitch. If I twitch a lot, it's likely I felt a strong emotion I didn't acknowledge. Often, that emotion is anger.

Or some nights, dreams hit me hard. I've always had a lot of dreams, but like most people, I wake up and the content slips away. I've learned to pay attention to what my subconscious wants to teach me. I have a recurring dream, for example, where I search for a place far from other people and sob uncontrollably. I get that message loud and clear. Even though my external outlook is optimistic, a deep part of me hasn't come to terms with my illness. At times, I still grieve my diagnosis.

This type of dream seems triggered when I miss out on something I would have enjoyed just months before, like skipping a friend's birthday cake. Everyone else had a piece, but I didn't allow myself even a bite of chocolatey goodness. My subconscious was sad about what life used to be.

That doesn't mean my conscious mind doesn't feel genuinely lucky to be alive. I've been saved from not just one calamity but two: physical and emotional. I'm more present in the moment than ever so in some deeply meaningful ways my life is better than before my illness. Yet a part of me disagrees. There are things about myself I find hard to admit by the light of day.

GETTING TO KNOW THE REAL ME

Clearly, my path to becoming whole in body, mind, and spirit continues. I have work to do.

My experience in Florida broke me, but once I started looking inside, I began to understand who I really am.

As I went through this journey, I found out what makes me tick. I gained insights into my past and the real me. Understanding my inner workings happens on three progressively deeper levels:

1. **Intellectual understanding:** This surface level was easy for me. I'm a thinker, and I saw no need to look deeper. But there's more to me than that. Knowing something in my head isn't enough to drive behavioral change.

2. **Emotional understanding:** This next level was harder, but my diagnosis jumpstarted a process of grappling with my emotions. Once I tapped into those feelings, I discovered I habitually ignored an enormous part of what goes on inside me.

3. **Visceral understanding:** This deepest level was the hardest, and I didn't even know it existed until my experience in Florida made me think I was losing everything. Visceral insight resides in our gut, and what we believe to be true in the core of our being drives how we think, feel, and act.

For all its wonderful moments, life can also be relentlessly harsh, unforgiving, and unlucky. To survive, we have no choice but to toughen up. While the protective armor we put on is incredibly helpful and might even save our lives, it can limit our awareness of who we really are. Physicist Richard Feynman said, "The first principle is that you must not fool yourself, and you are the easiest person to fool."

My armor made it easy to deceive myself about who I truly am, and the only way to discover the real me was to remove my protective shell. Little by little, the armor protecting the person I thought I was and which I presented to the world was stripped away.

This process was hard, and my mind resisted every step of the way. But discovering all the facts and feelings I buried deep inside has been one of the most valuable growth processes of my life. There are several things I now viscerally understand about myself:

- I didn't love myself.
- I devoted almost all my energy to my job.
- I didn't want to burden other people.
- I hated confrontation and conflict.

All those things add up to a guy who wanted to leave as little impact on the world as possible, someone I call "small Chris." This mindset probably made me a bad breather who never felt like he took in enough air. After all, it would be terrible to inhale more than my fair share of oxygen! How ridiculous, yet true.

This way of seeing myself goes way back. It's a coping mechanism I've cultivated since early childhood to manage stressful situations.

I'm the middle sibling. My older brother is mentally and physically handicapped and requires significant support. My younger sister was the girl my parents always wanted, and the family princess.

Not wanting to add to my parents' load, I did my utmost to be as self-sufficient as possible, never acted out, and always followed the rules. While my memory has no doubt faded, I only remember throwing a temper tantrum one time over a video game I really wanted. My rule-following ran so deep that I continually rejected offers from middle school friends to pay me $5 to utter a swear word. Any cuss word. My choice. I couldn't do it. As an adult, I've elevated swearing to an art. If the $5 offer was still open, I would be rich.

I always put on a happy face. Or at least one that said I was fine. I'm uncertain if I ever felt a negative emotion growing up, but if I did, I likely suppressed it long before it reached my consciousness.

In adulthood, my coping mechanisms expanded to include a lot of alcohol.

Like many, I "learned" to drink in college, and the habit continued into adulthood. I always enjoyed drinking with friends or coworkers, but over time, something more sinister emerged. I drank on Friday nights to help forget the stresses of the week. Tequila became my beverage of choice, and I explored countless brands before landing on Clase Azul as my favorite. As I assumed increasingly intense and prestigious roles at work, I did most of my Friday night drinking alone. It wasn't for fun. I needed it to release the stress I bottled up inside.

In retrospect, I realize I also used extreme exercise to cope with life's challenges. I usually worked out hard five to seven days a week. Sometimes I did two adays and drove myself to tackle very tough regimens. A healthy habit became an unhealthy obsession. I thought poorly of myself if I took a day off, and I never throttled back long enough for my body to adequately recover.

DRIVEN

This intense drive served me well through multiple crazy work settings into my mid-40s, including serving as interim CEO of a billion-dollar healthcare company. My coping mechanisms held strong until:

- I took a leadership role at a COVID testing company, and
- My mom passed.

Those events, occurring within 12 months of each other, were too great. My body broke, and my mind soon followed. Given the ability of cancer cells to rapidly multiply, that timeframe is likely when my immune system couldn't keep up, and cancer began growing inside me. Getting cancer in my intestines makes so much sense. It's where I buried all my negative emotions.

I'm moving forward in life knowing far more about myself. This new understanding empowers me to live authentically while caring for my own needs and loving others more fully. Here's a sample of what I've discovered.

I'M IMPATIENT

I want to move fast and get things done. This bias for action has served me well professionally because I've accomplished a lot when others couldn't, and I've repeatedly been rewarded with more responsibility. However, because I'm impatient, I always push myself and my teams to do more—and to do it faster, better, and cheaper. This relentlessness can burn out my team, and me.

A more subtle effect of my drive was my constant focus on what's next. I was so future forward that I was rarely in the present. When I was having a cocktail, I thought about the next cocktail. When I got the next cocktail, I thought about dinner. And as I ate dinner, I thought about dessert. I never truly enjoyed anything because my mind had already moved on.

Professionally, I was always strategizing what my colleagues and I could do next and was frequently upset at our current progress.

While this attribute helped propel me to high-level jobs, it left me wildly unhappy. I distinctly recall sitting in my office just weeks before I was diagnosed, feeling completely depressed about everything happening at work—or more accurately, everything not happening. I was spiraling downward with doubts about the future of the business. I let my worries take me down, which in retrospect, was ridiculous.

I'M A CONTROL FREAK

I had a simple metaphor to explain my mindset to my coworkers.

If a wine bottle is about to roll off a table,
I'm the guy who always reaches out
to stop it from falling off the table.

I applied this approach at work, frequently lunging out of my lane to ensure the proverbial wine bottle didn't shatter.

I did this frequently in the name of being a team player. While this behavior absolutely helped avoid bad situations and achieve greater success, it was exhausting. I gave so much of myself at work that there was little left for me or my family. Long ago, a mentor gave me advice I forgot until recently. He said, "Don't let someone else's passive become your active."

Said another way, just because someone is letting a wine bottle drop doesn't mean it's my job to jump up and save it. I leapt into action far too much. Frankly, my trying to control the outcomes of everything at work exposed my overblown pride. There are so many factors besides ME that determine a company's success or failure.

I conducted my personal life the same way. Arthur Brooks, best-selling author and professor of Management Practice at the Harvard Business School, stated on a Tim Ferriss podcast that everyone pursues one of four idols: money, power, pleasure, or fame. After much introspection, I realized I wanted power, and money was a vehicle to achieve that power.

When I was younger in my career, I wanted to be a CEO in no small part because I believed I would then call the shots, and the company would have to do what I thought was best. At the time, I didn't realize that a leader always reports to someone, in this case, the Board of Directors. I also wanted to be financially independent, again with the goal of controlling my destiny and never finding myself trapped in an undesirable situation. I now realize I chased money to have power in the form of total agency over my life. I worked incessantly to build the balance sheet so someday I wouldn't have to.

But as I learned with my diagnosis, that day might not ever come for me. Even then, I firmly believed that "My body helped create this cancer, so it can also help me heal it." With that control mindset, I radically remade my life to manage the outcome. While I still believe I have significant agency about my diagnosis, and I won't stop changing what I can. But at least I now understand I need help more than ever.

I'M A PEOPLE PLEASER

I hate conflict. I don't like thinking someone is mad at me, and I want everyone to like me. This disposition made me reluctant to raise my opinion for fear someone would disagree with me. I didn't want to debate, so I instead became adept at listening and mediating conflict. This became a highly valuable skill in healthcare, where a physician might be feuding with a technologist who is fighting with businesspeople. I found ways to lead cross-functional teams with seemingly opposite definitions of success. This superpower came at a huge cost. I frequently shut down my own perspective and suppressed the negative feelings that would naturally ensue.

Moreover, to keep others happy, I poured out so much of myself that there was no energy, safety net, or recovery left for me. This became obvious during the Florida retreat. How could I love myself if I suppressed the real me and gave away all my life energy?

I SHOULD BE ANGRY SOMETIMES

Throughout my many work roles, I've always received stellar feedback for my ability to stay calm under pressure. Team members said my ability to keep my composure freed them to express their thoughts and feelings even in tense situations. At the time, I thought my carefully practiced demeanor embodied the leadership principle that employees prefer predictable managers and dislike those who make them wonder what to expect, like the boss who is raging mad one day and all smiles the next. I took this point to heart and endeavored to maintain my calm confidence for the sake of my team.

I used the same approach at home. As a family, we prioritize eating dinner together whenever possible as a time to hear about each other's day. Unfortunately for me, I usually came straight from several hours of work with no time to decompress. If I were still processing a job issue, I might slam my fist on the table in frustration. When my family figured this out and made fun of me, I self-edited that behavior out of my dinnertime routine and added to the suppressed anger in my guts.

In both settings, I didn't realize I was leaving my anger unspoken and unprocessed. I simply buried my feelings, like hauling waste to a garbage dump and plowing it under. I let real and perceived slights stink inside me until my body couldn't take it anymore.

I'M TOO INDEPENDENT

Why rely on others when I can do it myself?

I believed that with enough perseverance, I could navigate any situation and overcome any obstacle. And I could do it without anyone else's help!

Growing up, I hated asking for help. I despised group projects. I even disliked sharing. I never wanted to owe a monetary, material, or emotional debt to anyone. I always declined things as trivial as accepting a handful of candy from a friend at the movies.

My steadfast independence continued until my diagnosis, when something intuitively clicked and made me realize there was no way I could overcome this alone. I went public with my diagnosis on LinkedIn. While I generally despise social media, that platform is where I have all my professional connections—along with a curated image of what I want everyone to see: a successful and up-and-coming healthcare executive. If I was going to heal my body, I'd need everyone who knew me and people who didn't to help me get there. This is one area where I've drastically changed. I no longer hesitate to ask for help.

GETTING MY ANGER OUT

Toward the end of December, Jing and I were out walking. She asked, "Are you angry at something or someone?" My kneejerk response was a firm no. If I was angry at anyone, it was me. I felt a sad fury at the person I had become and how my life choices possibly helped create the cancer. It wasn't until talk therapy and peer counseling gave me permission and power to explore my feelings that I realized I was still bitterly angry at a past boss. I thought I had forgiven him, but it was clear I had just said the words. I didn't feel them.

I found healing in an unexpected source. I listened over and over to a couple of songs that gave voice to my anger. They're anything but calm. The refrain of "Killing in the Name" by Rage Against the Machine felt like it was written about my old boss. As the band rocked on, I screamed right along. "Fuck you, I won't do what you tell me!"

Gone was the middle schooler who refused his friends' cash to cuss.

For reasons unknown at the time, I selected Metallica's "The Four Horsemen" as the complement to "Killing in the Name" and listened to these two songs whenever I went out for a drive. Jing and I were reading Dr. Peter Attia's book *Outlive*, which exposes what Attia called "the four horsemen of chronic disease." Several months earlier, I heard him mention in a podcast that these four conditions account for more than 80% of deaths in people over 50 who don't smoke: 1) atherosclerotic diseases like heart attacks and strokes, 2) cancer, 3) neurodegenerative diseases like Alzheimer's, and 4) foundational diseases, including type 2 diabetes.

As I quietly reflected on Attia's words, I realized the connection to the Metallica song I thought I randomly picked: "In the dead of night do the four horsemen ride, they've come to take your life." Whoa. My subconscious put all these pieces together from a podcast months earlier to help me address my rage over the cancer diagnosis. My spine still tingles when I realize the mind's power.

I planned to take this process of purging my anger a step further by reenacting a scene from the movie *Office Space* where employees vent their professional frustrations by destroying a printer with a baseball bat. I already had a bat, and I found a printer ready to meet its doom. But by then, all my internal work had significantly cleared my pent-up rage, and the printer still sits in pristine condition in my garage. The fact that it remains in one piece is evidence of my progress.

SPEAKING MY TRUTH

I had many tough nights as I weaned from sleep meds. I couldn't unwind enough to fall asleep. Or I would wake up in the wee hours and be on high alert for hours. Or my twitching feet would make me lose my mind. One particularly unsettled night, I was so uncomfortable I went to our guest bedroom to try again. I wasn't sure why I felt so off, but I started talking softly to myself about everything I was thinking and feeling. At some point, I said aloud, "I just need to write the damn book!" I repeated it a few times, and it felt incredibly right. My mind settled, and I drifted off to sleep.

It became obvious what drove my agitation. A book had been on my bucket list, but I never had a topic I thought was worth sharing. Early in the diagnosis, I wrote an outline, but even that felt inconsequential. Over time, however, I realized I was traveling a unique path and could potentially help others. That night my mind committed to writing these words, and I recognize now that my spirit and subconscious had been leading the way.

A few days later, I went to my weekly acupuncture session. My amazing practitioner helps me as much with making sense of my thoughts as with healing my body. I told her all about the four horsemen, and she was thrilled I made the connections. I also shared that I felt compelled to write a book.

"You want to hear something equally crazy?" she asked. She said that during my last appointment, she placed the needles and was about to shut the door when she heard a deep voice say, "He is going to write a book." The voice was so loud she almost opened the door to ask if I heard it. As I told her my plans, she smiled and said she already knew. Whoa.

OFFICE HOURS

As I work through my emotions, it helps me greatly to talk with others. I also find it healing to converse with myself. Really!

I've mentioned meeting with a Brown University professor who specializes in recovery from bad meditation outcomes. As a survivor of similar experiences, she holds "office hours" with her earlier selves to process her past, which is often the first step to moving on. One night when I was having trouble sleeping, I intentionally declared office hours with myself. I was amazed at the childhood memories that flooded my brain. Almost all involved me playing—with my dad, my sister, my grandparents, but also by myself. The memories were pleasant, but I was also startled by how much I did alone. Today, I'm still a kid at heart. I love to play almost any game, real or made-up. These insights reminded me how critical play is to my happiness.

This happy realization convinced me I had emptied the reservoir of negative emotions my body was holding. There was no rush of anger, no sadness, just play and fun. Holding office hours with myself is yet another tool I use when I fall out of balance.

What could office hours look like for you? Or what else might help you go deeper into the real you? Are you getting a sense of what makes you tick? What armor do you wear? What mechanisms do you deploy to protect yourself from the words and actions that hurt more than you want to admit? Can you identify bottled-up thoughts or emotions you need to get out?

We all need toughness just to survive the day with family, coworkers, and "friends." Nevertheless, there's no better time to get past that shell and really understand who you are. Be brutally honest. Go beyond intellectual and emotional understanding. Go for the visceral!

That deep level of self-examination will be uncomfortable. It might even trigger past traumatic incidents, so I recommend you undertake this effort with professional support. But don't shy away from doing the work. On the other side of the revelations, you will know yourself, love yourself, live authentically, and become a beacon for others to do the same.

This inner journey will bring you more love and fulfillment than you can imagine.

As I write this book, I feel as naked and exposed as the day I was born. I'm disclosing who I am without any armor or protection. People will now know exactly what sticks and stones to throw at me that will really break me. While I feel vulnerable sharing my weak points, it's also incredibly liberating. I'm done putting energy into maintaining my got-it-together external image. My reclaimed energy fuels me to write these words.

I now feel so much happier and more fulfilled than ever before. I now know me. I now love me!

CHAPTER 19:

REMISSION—AND MUCH MORE

In late January, I got a PET scan which—unlike an MRI or CT—shows whether cancer cells are active. I had shied away from this test because it requires injecting radioactive glucose, the favorite food of cancer cells. Why do potential harm to my body unless it was absolutely necessary?

My oncologist expressed confidence that the test would be positive, in large part because the spots on my intestine had completely disappeared. I was likewise confident, basing my belief that the cancer was gone due to my breakthroughs at the meditation retreat. I remained certain all would be well until the night before the scan. I told myself I shouldn't be surprised—and I would still be okay—if a few spots showed up.

I went to bed feeling more excited than anxious to see what the test would say, but my nerves were enough to disrupt my sleep that night. When I checked in for the test the following morning, an 86-year-old stood in line ahead of me. My instant thought was Dang, good for you that you made it to that age and can get a PET scan. I'm sure he was thinking more like I was. I just want some more time on this earth.

The PET scan was pleasant. I sat alone in a dark room for an hour before the actual test. It was nice to be without my phone, with just my thoughts keeping me company. The test was over before I knew it.

Later that day, I got a fateful email notifying me that the test results were in. This was the moment of truth. Would the cancer really be gone?

At that moment, my whole existence was wrapped up in that email. Was my body really healed? Would I get a second chance? What did my future hold?

I had envisioned Jing and me sitting at the kitchen island as I opened the message on my iPad. The scene played out exactly as I had pictured, except that we headed downstairs. I didn't want our daughters nearby if the news was bad.

Our eyes rapidly scanned the report. The previous results were detailed to the point of being difficult to understand, but this message was unequivocal: My body had a "complete response to treatment." Jing and I locked eyes, embraced, and held each other as we cried tears of pure joy. I said "Thank you, Jesus," again and again. We went upstairs to tell the girls the great news and spent the rest of the evening video chatting with the close family members and friends who had been with us every step of this arduous journey.

Everyone asked how I felt. My response oddly resembled my initial diagnosis. I felt nothing. More precisely, I didn't know what to think. I was relieved the report confirmed what I believed to be true, but I didn't feel the pure elation I expected. Maybe I had been convinced of my healing for so long that it was hard to feel surprised.

A few days later, we met with my local oncologist. Jing had grown nervous that he might say something different despite her having Googled every word of the report and getting confirmations from my physician friends that we had read the results correctly. My oncologist completely agreed that the news meant what we thought. He pulled up the scan images and said they indicated no cell activity. "Congratulations!" he confidently stated. "You're in remission!"

With a Stage 4 diagnosis, there's always a concern about rogue cancer cells still circulating in the body. The standard response is to continue taking Gleevec forever. Unsurprisingly, my oncologist affirmed this recommendation. While Jing had found studies that said pairing Gleevec with another medicine could do even better, searching out and destroying bad cells, for now, my oncologist recommended against that possible step.

OR NOT?

My wife and I have a straightforward relationship with my oncologist, and he supported our intention of getting another perspective from a national center of excellence. We had found a center with experts specific to my cancer, but we concluded it would take weeks to get on their schedule. I decided to message a center we had already visited. I wanted to know their thoughts about the best ways to wipe out cells that might be hiding in my system, and I was eager to get going on the next steps.

I couldn't contact the doctor directly, forcing me to communicate through the patient portal. I sent a message about my clean PET scan and remission, adding that I wanted to discuss options for further treatment. I heard nothing for days until the portal notified me that three appointments had been added to my personal calendar. Great—but what the heck?

I reached back to a nurse via the portal. She said they wanted to do an MRI to get a better look at my liver. When I asked why, I again got silence. I finally reached the nurse live, and she reinforced the need for the MRI and seemed exasperated by my persistent questioning. If I declined the MRI, their radiologist would reread the PET scan, a service I would have to pay for out of pocket. Again—really? Many thousands of dollars to reread a PET scan? I felt like I was being shaken down. What's more, this renowned center of excellence completely ignored my initial question. Why did I need the MRI at all?

It felt like I had gone to a restaurant and ordered a cheeseburger. Someone in the kitchen rejected my order and sent out a steak. If I refused the steak, they were poised to force-feed me surf-and-turf. Why does US healthcare do this?

My wife and I were very conflicted, like a wet blanket was thrown over our exceptionally positive news. Did they know something we didn't? My local oncologist thought the spots on my liver were probably holes that might close with time. Did he miss something? I wished I had never inquired in the first place and wanted to reject their demands. I asked for my local oncologist's perspective, hoping he would tell me to quit while I could.

My physician admitted the situation was "very awkward." While the MRI was likely unnecessary, he recommended I go ahead in case the clinic someday conducts a trial I wanted to participate in. It seemed like the wrong reason to get yet another scan. Yet, the lingering doubt the center had created coupled with my desire to keep options open prodded us forward.

Working with the center of excellence required two days, one for the scan and another to meet with the physician. I mentally started girding myself for the MRI, the worst option among cancer tests. With my nose two inches away from a machine that whirs and clanks like something from Charlie and the Chocolate Factory, I would need to lay still for a couple of hours. At this center, there was no heated blanket, cushion under my knees, or soothing choice of music pumped into headphones. All I got here were clanks and thuds.

The physician meeting the next day was our chance to finally understand what the hell was going on. I said I was confused as to why more tests were necessary when I was now in remission.

The doctor flatly stated that while my response to the drugs was amazing, I wasn't in remission. Wait a minute. What?!?

The doctor went on to declare that no one diagnosed with Stage 4 can ever be in remission because cancer cells might still be circulating in the body at a level too low for current tests to pick up. She pointed out that all 15 spots on my liver remained largely unchanged since my last scan. This news was unbelievably deflating, yet she told me multiple times, "You should be thrilled with this result."

So were the cells in my liver dead—or not?

Cancer is all about numbers. The more cells, the higher the chance of mutation. The higher the chance of mutation, the higher the risk that drugs won't do their thing, and I ultimately die. According to the doctor, the MRI indicated the spots were likely dead, but we couldn't be sure. All we knew for certain was that they weren't "metabolically active" at a rate the PET scan could detect.

For reference, one of those spots likely contained millions if not billions of cancer cells, and I still had 15 of them. I would feel A LOT better about my chances if I had a handful of cancer cells floating through my body than millions or billions lying dormant and waiting to start multiplying again. The doctor tried again to assuage my fears by saying again, "You should be thrilled with the result." She stopped short of saying the cells were dead because the only way to be sure was to biopsy them, and that wasn't worth the risk.

We ended the appointment with me faking being thrilled.

"Remission" as defined by the
National Cancer Institute:
A decrease in or disappearance
of signs and symptoms of cancer.

In partial remission, some but not all signs and symptoms of cancer are gone. In complete remission, all signs and symptoms of cancer have disappeared, although cancer may still be in the body.

My wife and I headed home, a few hours when we would normally rehash everything we had heard. But I couldn't do it. I was a numb little bug. I didn't want to talk. I didn't know what to think. My wife took the visit better than I did and prodded me to engage, but it was evident I had turned inward. I was sad. Disappointed. Wishing I had never reached out. Regretting I hadn't rejected the visit.

I was no longer sure I had been given a second chance.

I understood that the clinic doctor thought she was doing the right thing by providing me with the most precise assessment of my health possible. She wouldn't go beyond stating my cancer "wasn't metabolically active at this time."

So what's the big deal? I felt like the people who were supposed to help attempted to take a word away from me for the rest of my life. In their singular quest for precision, they obliterated the word "remission."

At what cost?

Hope. Hope that remission is possible. The hope my body requires in order to heal. If I don't believe healing is possible, then by default, it isn't.

Hope got me to this point, and I as sure as hell wasn't going to give it up.

NEW NORMAL—AND MORE

Over the following months, the self-realizations slowed to a trickle, and I was blessed that life could largely return to "normal."

I remained steadfast in my belief that the cancer was indeed completely gone, and I was given a second chance at life.

I encountered my first hiccup in November 2024 when I got E. coli food poisoning, likely from my favorite sushi restaurant in Columbia, Maryland. Knowing we had put so much energy into getting my gut biome healthy, I resisted taking traditional antibiotics and instead took diatomaceous earth daily. Yes, there actually is food-grade diatomaceous earth made from a soft rock composed of fossilized remains of tiny aquatic organisms. I had previously only used the substance to kill deer ticks at our cabin. While my symptoms intermittently improved, it was clear I couldn't shake the food poisoning, so after a month I gave in and took traditional antibiotics. This gave me a couple of weeks of respite.

However, around the holidays, I started each morning with such intense pain in my rectum that I can only describe it as a "charley horse." Luckily the pain didn't last long, but there was no going back to sleep after that happened. For the next several weeks I continued to experience a variety of abdominal pains, a persistent dull ache on my left side, shooting pain in my stomach, and the morning charley horse wake-up call.

In addition, an intense bout of neck pain prevented me from

embarking on my first work trip of the new year. This sounds eerily like what was happening before my initial diagnosis, but unfortunately, I was blind to this at the time. That was in part because I went to my PCP, who ordered a CT scan primarily to check for diverticulitis which also gave me a checkpoint on the presence of any new spots. Surprisingly, the CT came back negative on both fronts, so I was referred to a gastroenterologist (GI doctor). I wasn't supposed to get a scan for another three months, so I was elated that the scan was clear. I wouldn't need another scan until late July, so I could keep planning for the future.

The GI doctor thought my traumatized intestines were sending unwarranted pain signals to my brain. He said this could go on for months, even a year! Medication could possibly help with the symptoms but would do nothing for the underlying problem. Reluctantly, I got the prescription, hesitant to add to an increasingly long list of daily pills.

Luckily my symptoms simply went away in February, and life seemed to return to normal.

BOARD MEETING

Due to my GI issues and random neck pain, I had to cancel every work trip since the beginning of the year. Our corporate board meeting was coming up, and there was no way I was going to miss this important trip as I was presenting an entirely new product/service to the board.

However, just two days before I was scheduled to fly out, all the assorted pains in my abdomen returned. I had intense gas build-up but couldn't pass gas, the persistent dull ache on my left side continued to wear me down, and random shooting pains were icing on the cake. None of this was going to stop me from going. Adding yet another degree of difficulty, Minnesota was under a winter weather advisory and expected to get several inches of snow, putting my 6:50 AM departure at risk.

Not to be deterred, I got up at 4:00 AM and rolled around my bathroom floor to pass as much gas as possible. Anyone looking would have seen a man-sized baby rolling around and grabbing his toes.

For once, the weatherman hadn't oversold the storm. There was indeed a lot of snow on the ground, and blizzard conditions developed as it continued to snow and blow. It was one of my most challenging, white-knuckled drives ever. Several times I had to accelerate so my Mini Cooper could clear the inches of snow the plow left at an intersection. I was lucky to reach the airport safely.

I arrived at the gate on time, but unsurprisingly, the flight was delayed four hours. I searched for a place where I could lie down and catch a little sleep. As I came in and out of a light nap, it was clear my stomach pain was growing worse. As the hours wore on, my flight was delayed another two hours. By that point, I had missed the entire day of meetings and still might be challenged to make the actual board meeting. The pain had become so severe I couldn't stand up straight, and I finally asked myself, "What the hell am I doing?" I reluctantly called the CEO and told him I was deeply apologetic, but I couldn't make the meeting. In hindsight, it feels obvious that neither God nor my body wanted me to get on that plane, and after a multitude of signs, my thick-headed brain got the message.

I pulled out of the airport ramp and drove directly to urgent care. Given I could barely walk, they strongly recommended I get a CT scan. They believed I had an abscess in my intestines. I wanted as few CT scans as possible to limit radiation and damage to my kidneys, and every CT scan felt like I might be giving up years of my life to feel better in the present moment. It wasn't a trivial decision. I started to cry just at the prospect of saying yes.

The results of the CT scan completely stunned me. The cancer had returned, and in milliseconds, the word "remission" evaporated.

Not only was it back, but the spot was quite large, accompanied by several peritoneal nodules. Only five weeks had passed since the last clear CT scan. How could my condition have gone so bad so fast? What would have happened if I had waited five more months for a scan?

As reality hit, I started sobbing uncontrollably. The unfortunate nurse practitioner who delivered the news was an amazing human and tried to comfort me as best he could. I was devastated.

Whenever I had discussed the possibility of reoccurrence with the oncologist, he said a small spot could appear and then disappear. If it didn't disappear he could go in and remove or ablate the stubborn spot. It felt much more like a chronic condition I would have to manage. Even if that meant dealing with the issue for years, I felt entirely optimistic about the future. This latest CT scan was the exact opposite, seeming to suggest I might have mere months if we didn't figure out how to address it.

Still in pain and teary-eyed, I drove home to see Jing. I could barely get the words out as I started sobbing again. So many thoughts flooded my brain: We did everything the first time—what now? I didn't deviate from my diet, mindfulness, or exercise plan—why did this happen? It was so hard the first time—how are we going to do this again? If cancer was going to come back, why didn't it come back like they said it would? I still have so much more good I can do—God, why did this come back? The last thought turned into a shout and lingered far after the rest—what if I have no agency over whether I survive this time?

Emotionally I was a wreck, and physically the pain was getting worse by the hour. Even OxyContin provided no relief. I was in so much pain I couldn't walk ten steps to go to the bathroom without my wife's assistance. Just 72 hours earlier, I thought I was completely healthy. Jing and I had just completed a 4.5-mile walk, with me loaded up with my 50-pound rucksack. How could my life fall apart so quickly?

We decided there was no option but to go to the emergency room. After waiting for what felt like an eternity, I got a room, and they started administering pain medication. This was the only time I can remember that I rated my pain a 10 out of 10. Luckily, this new pain medication started to provide relief. I thought for sure they would admit me, but after a few doses of pain medication, they sent us home at 2am.

THE AFTERMATH

Given how quickly the cancer was progressing, my wife and I had no option but to spring into action. On the Western medicine front, the oncologist doubled the dose of my chemotherapy pill, and we scheduled a surgical consultation. Meanwhile, we reached out to a center of excellence in Florida to get an appointment while starting the arduous process of submitting records there as well as to the NIH for a clinical surgical trial. On the alternative medicine front, we tried to find a local naturopathic physician. Just as before, this became a full-time job for my wife and me.

THE NEW GAME PLAN

Fortunately, with the double dose of the chemotherapy pill, the pain subsided so we didn't need to pursue emergency surgery. However, it wasn't lost on me that the new large spot came back right by the original spot. I wanted it all removed. We were lucky to get surgery scheduled at the NIH with a surgical oncologist who only focuses on GIST cancer. We completely changed my diet—again—cutting all grains for multiple reasons and adding a small amount of fish to ensure I got all the trace minerals I needed. We found a naturopathic provider we liked with expertise in natural cancer treatments and began to augment my body with a raft of supplements and treatments.

Candidly, we changed so much at once that it didn't all go smoothly. I was low on magnesium, but the double dose of magnesium caused a painful stomachache in the middle of the night. I was also taking an extremely high dose of melatonin (200mg) to slow tumor growth, but no matter when I took this, it left me feeling like a complete zombie and started to cause kidney pain. After a few weeks, my body was feeling the full effects of a double dose of chemotherapy. Doing anything as simple as walking up a flight of stairs, emptying the dishwasher, or folding clothes left me completely out of breath. I started to wonder if all these treatments would kill me before the cancer did.

This point really hit home after I got IV vitamin C treatment and the next day went for a routine appointment with my oncologist. After giving blood, I began to feel super weird: My brain slowed, I became nauseous, my body started to shiver, and I felt like reality was slipping through my fingers. Evidently, my hemoglobin had dropped to 6.0. Normal levels for an adult male are 14.0-17.5, and anything below 8.0 is so concerning that you need a blood transfusion.

They rushed me to the hospital in an ambulance—my fourth time—so I could start getting the much-needed transfusions. Three units of blood over two days was enough for me to return home.

To get a vitamin C infusion, I first needed a G6PD test to ensure the vitamin C wouldn't damage red blood cells. It's believed this is a genetic test—meaning it doesn't change and doesn't need to be done more than once. However, Jing found research that indicated the number could possibly change and that chemotherapy could impact it. No one had told us this, and my low hemoglobin now made sense. It was likely already low from the double dose of chemotherapy; the IV vitamin C probably pushed it even lower, beyond the point where my body could function.

Herein lies a cautionary tale. We want so much to heal ourselves, but no doctor has the expertise to understand how all the changes might interact in positive or potentially deadly ways. Moreover, in our current healthcare system, no collection of doctors interacts in a way that they might have a shot at putting all the clues together. The more adept you are at listening to your body, the better your chance of realizing what helps versus hurts. Remember, most providers only get 10 or 20 minutes a month to think about your health. If you're in a situation like mine, you spend almost infinitely more time thinking about your health. Don't discount that investment and your own ability to spot difficulties no one else can see.

THE SURGERY

Jing and I arrived in Bethesda, Maryland, on Sunday evening. Although the surgery wasn't scheduled until Thursday, I needed to undergo three days of pre-op testing. We couldn't stay at the National Institutes of Health (NIH) until I was admitted, so we found a Marriott a few minutes away.

NIH

NIH is an intimidating facility. Guards stand watch at every gate, and visitors exit their vehicle and put all their belongings through a metal detector while their car is thoroughly inspected. Since our first appointment was 6am on Monday, we took an Uber which dropped us off in front of security. Once we cleared security we had to walk a fair distance uphill to reach the building. The walk was pretty exhausting, and Jing could tell I wasn't doing great.

All the pre-op testing is self-service, meaning we received a daily schedule with rough guidance on locations, and it was up to us to get to the right place at the right time. The cryptic instructions combined with the size of the building intimidated both of us.

We saw my surgeon later in the day and found my hemoglobin had dropped yet again, which at least explained my trouble walking uphill. With Jing's encouragement, I got yet another blood transfusion that afternoon so I wouldn't crash right before the surgery.

Over the next few days, we completed all my pre-op tests and everything was a go. I learned that if the surgeon needed to remove part of my rectum I could end up with a colostomy bag for the rest of my life. I hadn't been aware of this possibility, and the prospect definitely scared me. I was admitted to the hospital on Wednesday afternoon. I wondered if I would start feeling anxious or worried before the surgery. But I surprised myself; I was quite the opposite. I was calm and even excited we had finally arrived at the day that seemed so far away when it was initially scheduled.

SURGERY DAY

Everything in the hospital starts early, generally between 4 and 5 am. Surgery day was no exception, with a flurry of activity to get everything ready. My memory of the day is mostly a blur. I recall there was trouble inserting the epidural for pain management. I was scheduled to recover in the Intensive Care Unit (ICU) due to the invasiveness of the surgery, but as I came out of anesthesia, I discovered I was in the Post-Anesthesia Care Unit (PACU). I was groggy but pleasantly surprised. It meant I would head back to my room instead of the ICU. Surgery must have gone well!

As I became more aware of my condition, I felt like Pinocchio, with at least four IVs stuck into both arms, another line for the epidural, a catheter, and most painful of all, a nasogastric (NG) tube pumping my stomach. It was a lot.

At some point, I learned my surgery was a success. The big reason I didn't end up in the ICU was that my liver, rectum, and everything above my pelvis was clean!

The surgery required over seven hours to remove:

- My appendix, which had a growth on it.
- Meckel's Diverticulum, a genetic birth defect for which my younger sister already had emergency surgery to address.
- Part of my small intestine, location of the primary tumor.
- The largest tumor, which was separate from the primary and located at the base of my pelvis. I later learned the surgeon named this tumor "Medusa" due to its unsightly appearance. (Check the Appendix if you want to confirm that for yourself. Not for the squeamish.)
- More than 80 tumors across my peritoneal sac.

Among everything I wasn't expecting, the most startling was the 80+ tumors removed. Going into surgery, we were expecting to remove the primary, the pelvic mass, and maybe a few peritoneal tumors. Post-surgery, I was grateful to God we went to the NIH for the surgery and didn't rush to have it done locally. I'm not sure anyone else would have done a seven-hour surgery AND had the expertise to complete it successfully. The surgeon was highly confident he got everything. We were elated!

It's now clear to me I needed this surgery to live. Just as Dr. Marvin Henson saved my mind in Florida after the meditation retreat, Dr. Andrew Blakely and his team saved my body. I call him my "Angel in Maryland" and I'm so grateful he was willing to do the surgery.

THE RECOVERY

I anticipated the recovery would be tough, but what does "tough" mean? What would it feel like? Unfortunately, a few of the nurses set unrealistic expectations for me by saying "Every day would get better." This was absolutely not the case. I never knew what was in store on any given day, or especially any particular night.

My third night was the most physically challenging of my life. At this point, I was still connected to multiple IVs, an epidural, and a catheter—but luckily, no stomach pump. As I tried to go to sleep, I felt intense gas pain. I didn't know at the time that an epidural doesn't really help with gas pain. I laid in bed staring at the clock as minutes ticked by. I didn't know what to do. As the night wore on, I still couldn't sleep, and the gas pain worsened. Around 2 am, I convinced the nurse to give me additional pain medication (Dilaudid, also known as hydromorphone).

I thought I would finally be able to catch a few hours of sleep, but less than 45 minutes after the injection, I experienced breakthrough pain, a pain that spiked so quickly I immediately worried I was in deep trouble.

Doing some physical gymnastics with all the tubes, I was able to get into a mix between downward dog and child's pose yoga positions on my hospital bed. My untied gown dropped away, and the sight of my bare butt high in the air must have looked ridiculous to the nurses. But the shooting pain was less severe in this position, so I stayed that way for hours. I skipped sleep because the alternative of screaming shooting pain seemed worse.

In that moment, I felt I was breaking before God's eyes.

I wasn't sure how I was going to
get through the next 15 minutes.
I wasn't sure I wanted to.
I realized I was only going to get
through if I gave control to God.

The first verse of the Casting Crowns song "Be Held" perfectly captures what I was going through:

Hold it all together
Everybody needs you strong
But life hits you out of nowhere
And barely leaves you holding on

And when you're tired of fighting
Chained by your control
There's freedom in surrender
Lay it down and let it go

(Chorus)

So when you're on your knees and answers seem so far away
You're not alone, stop holding on and just be held
Your world's not falling apart, it's falling into place
I'm on the throne, stop holding on and just be held

I cry every time I hear this song. As I reflect, it feels like I was born again that night.

I stayed in the hospital another 10 days and endured plenty of additional pains. I'm not sure there's much value for me or you in elaborating on everything that happened, but here are glimpses of the daily struggle:

- I didn't shower for 14 days.
- I frequently slept no more than two to four hours a night for 13 days.
- I was unable to wear normal clothes for 13 days.
- I didn't eat solid food for over 10 days.
- I was largely unable to brush my teeth for nine days due to the stomach pump in my nose.
- Maybe not surprisingly, I had no interest in my phone or anything happening outside the walls of my hospital room.

In the above state, I realized how much dopamine I normally receive on a normal day as well as the cortisol I craved to get through the day—normal body chemicals from amazingly simple things:

- Being able to take a hot shower.
- The taste of hot coffee or tea in the morning.
- Dressing in clothes that make me feel good.
- Deciding what I want to eat throughout the day.
- Opening my phone for a social media dopamine hit.

I could go on and on about all the good we experience on an average day. But my surgery and its aftermath helped me realize that I often take those things for granted. It's easy to feel unhappy and conclude the bad days outweigh the good. But when everything is taken away, I just dreamed about how good a hot shower would feel or how good some freshly cooked eggs would taste.

I hope people will take this nudge to pause and reflect on how lucky most of us are most of the time. If we aren't experiencing physical or mental pain, our average day is likely pretty darn good. But we need to create space in our frenetic schedule to let ourselves slow down and take it all in. Yes, we all have problems to deal with. Always. Some are very serious. But as we consider our whole context, the problems are likely smaller than we think.

I urge you to make moments to recognize the many things you do have, and everything you get to do. We are far more blessed than we realize!

I labored through 13 days before I was finally ready for discharge and able to travel home to Minnesota. I know my road to recovery will take many months and the future is uncertain. Yet, I left the hospital with the most important acronym possible:

NED

No Evidence of Disease

PART 3: YOUR HOW-TO GUIDE

CHAPTER 20:
PREPARATION

It's my deepest wish that you or a loved one never get a call like I did that Friday afternoon informing me I had Stage 4 cancer. Unfortunately, if you're reading this book, that's likely not the case. I'm sorry for what you and those around you are going through. Your world has changed forever. Once the "C" word has touched you, there's no putting it back in the bottle.

> ***In the following pages,***
> ***I offer practical insights to***
> ***help you during your journey.***
> ***What lies ahead is difficult—***
> ***but not insurmountable.***

To make this content more actionable, I break my learnings into three sections: preparation (chapter 20), diagnosis (chapter 21), and treatment (chapter 22). This structure allows you to rapidly access the insights you need at your point in the journey. I aim to be concise and refer to just a handful of trusted sources to support my recommendations.

The information provided here represents my experiences as a layperson, along with the thoughts of others who have gone through similar travails. What I share should not be taken as medical advice. This is one educated human's path to healing. I invite you to use what makes sense to you and throw away the rest.

I wish you Godspeed on your journey and am sending PEP (Prayers, Energy and Positivity) to you, your family, and everyone in your support system!

FIND THE RIGHT PRIMARY CARE PROVIDER (PCP)

Maybe artificial intelligence (AI) will change this dynamic in the future, but for now your primary care provider (PCP) is your key medical resource and guide, and there's no way around the fact that choosing that person can be a tough decision. If all goes well, you will interact with your PCP for a very long time. Your well-being demands an open and transparent relationship. Ask yourself:

1. Do I have a primary care provider?
2. If yes, when was my last annual physical?
3. If yes for both questions, do I like and trust my PCP?

If you answered "no" to any of these questions, it's crucial to search now for a physician who will take time with you to listen well and consider all the variables that make you a unique individual.

Years ago when I lived in California and had high calcium in my blood, my PCP initiated a text string with multiple specialists to figure out the cause. While that situation was unusual, my doctor clearly cared about me and did his utmost to get to the root of my problem. The last thing you want is a doctor whose highest priority seems to be rushing through appointments and filling out CPT codes (Current Procedural Terminology) to maximize insurance billings.

The search for a new PCP can be challenging for several reasons:

1. You need to **find out which PCPs are in your insurer network.** The fastest path to this information is logging onto your insurer's website and selecting "Find a Provider."

   Some insurance plans require you to select a PCP during enrollment or simply assign a PCP, meaning you might have a doctor you have never even met. Schedule time with that person as soon as possible. If your PCP isn't a match, switch to another.

2. Within the network, **check which PCPs are accepting new patients.** Many of the better PCPs are at capacity and can't accept new patients. Ask to be put on a waitlist.

3. **Consider more than travel time.** Finding a PCP in your immediate neighborhood shouldn't be your only filter. Barring serious mobility issues, the right provider is worth extra minutes in the car. Your visits will hopefully be infrequent, and many providers offer video appointments after an initial meeting. Focus on finding the best partner for your long-term health.

4. If you feel unsatisfied with your network options, **investigate concierge PCP practices.** Although concierge physicians charge an annual fee for more access, don't exclude this option without weighing the cost and benefits. I interviewed multiple PCPs before selecting the one who was right for me.

If you choose a concierge practice, confirm that they will bill your insurance directly. If the answer is "yes," check if the PCP is in-network. If not, your insurance will bill your visits as out-of-network, which can get expensive very quickly. One caveat: My PCP wasn't listed as in-network, but the office address was. The insurance company said my visits would be billed in-network, but I worried about it until the first bill confirmed that fact.

To the degree you intend to pursue alternative treatments, your risk of a strained relationship with your physician increases, especially if that person takes the approach of "my way or the highway."

Remember, you don't need your doctor's permission to explore other treatments. You do want to make that person aware of your choices in case anything might negatively impact your traditional treatment protocol (e.g., contraindications).

Honestly, I believe any negative energy in the doctoring process is so unhelpful to your healing that I would recommend changing physicians if they aren't on the same page with your treatment plan. Your diagnosis inevitably requires you to have tough conversations with your doctor. Layering interpersonal conflict on top can make the relationship unsustainable. Once you have a sense of how you will approach healing your body, start talking with your PCP sooner rather than later to confirm you're a match.

GET BLOOD WORK

I was shocked to discover that not all blood panels are equal. So basic to assessing your health, but such a mess to understand.

When my oncologist took blood for the "Standard Metabolic Panel" that revealed my elevated liver levels, I immediately wondered if those markers had been high a few months earlier at my annual physical. I soon realized that my previous "Standard Metabolic Panel" lacked markers for liver health. Even more curious, the "Standard Metabolic Panel" at a different executive physical included one marker for liver function but omitted two others. So I had three Standard Metabolic Panels from three PCPs, and they were all different!

I incorrectly assumed that "Standard" meant standard across providers. Takeaway: If you're going to undergo bloodwork once a year, make sure the panel includes all the significant markers to catch any early warning signals. Below is a table of potentially applicable tests and the minimum I would ensure your provider includes in your Standard Metabolic Panel:

PANEL	TARGET	MEASURE	LAYPERSON COMMENTS
Comprehensive Metabolic Panel	Kidney	Bun	Should correlate with creatinine
	Kidney	Creatinine	Should use Cystatin C if this is high
	Kidney	GFR	Know that GFR can be calculated in three ways if low
	Diabetes	Glucose	Useful to check the continuous glucose monitor (CGM) against this value
	Calcium	Calcium Serum	If high, find out why to make sure calcium isn't leaching from your bones
	Protein for Vegans	Albumin	Should stay at 4.0 or above
	Liver	Alkaline Phosphatase	
	Liver	AST	
	Liver	ALT	
CBC/ Differential OP	Immune System	LYMPHOCYTE ABSOLUTE OP	All different measures of the immune system; Naturopathic note: If considering mistletoe therapy, your eosinophil percentage should be below 6%
		MONOCYTE ABSOLUTE OP	
		EOSINOPHIL ABSOLUTE OP	
		BASOPHIL ABSOLUTE OP	
	Anemia	Red blood cell count	Likely to be low if undergoing treatment, important that it remains stable
		Hemoglobin	
		Hematocrit	
NA	Kidney	Cystatin C (will include GFR reading)	Better measure for the kidneys
Lipid Panel	Heart	Cholesterol	
		HDL	
		LDL	
NA	Heart	Coronary artery calcium (CAC) score	Better predictor than cholesterol for heart disease

PANEL	TARGET	MEASURE	LAYPERSON COMMENTS
NA	Heart	Serum Ceramide	Not frequently prescribed, but a unique blood marker for heart health
NA	Immune System	Vitamin D	Recommended to be at the top end of the range
NA	Anemia	Vitamin B12	Critical for producing red blood cells
NA	Diabetes	Hemoglobin A1C	Should correlate with glucose if tracking that
NA	Diabetes	Fasting Insulin	A better measure of earlier metabolic issues than A1C for risk of diabetes and cardiac issues
NA	Immune System	Copper	Overall immune system, naturopathic measure. Level and ratio are important between copper/zinc
NA	Immune System	Zinc	
NA	IV Vitamin C	G6PD	Determines whether you can receive IV vitamin C, a genetic measure that only needs to be taken once. If your hemoglobin is low, I would ask for a rapid test as I believe this can change over time (I likely ended up in the hospital as a result of this situation).

UNDERSTAND YOUR BLOODWORK

Most patients will discover that their bloodwork results show a mix of high and low levels. If you're like me, the numbers and graphs will send cortisol racing through your veins, and you will spend hours furiously searching online for the precise meaning of each result.

This happened to me during my most recent annual physical. The normal range for a common thyroid test was listed as between 0.358 – 3.74. My value was 5.809. The graph presented this value to the far right, which made me think my result was extremely high, and I immediately began to worry I suffered from hypothyroidism.

However, my physician said my level was only moderately high,

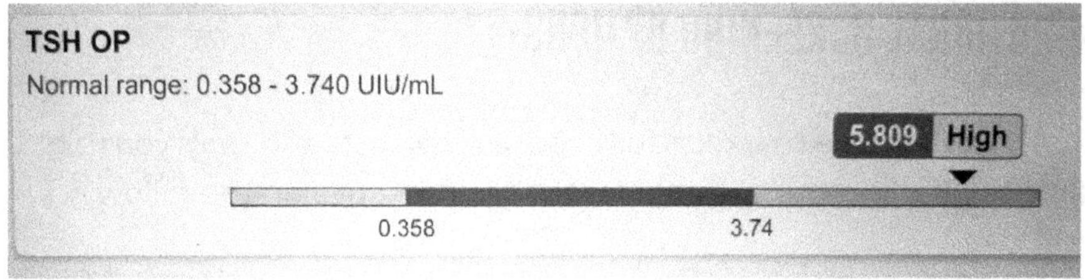

and it would take a result of 10 or even 20 to cause concern. The graph in my report didn't even cover that range.

It's also important to understand what constitutes a statistically significant difference on a blood test. For example, my hemoglobin was 6.0 at the oncology office but 6.4 just an hour later in the emergency room. For this specific test, values within 0.5 are treated the same. It's another important variable to understand before you get too worried or excited about your latest lab values.

Takeaway: It's crucial to understand what constitutes truly high or low for a test before self-diagnosing an issue.

Adding to the confusion, healthcare providers stake out different ranges of what they consider high or low. At the same physical, I was also tested for lipoprotein (A), a measure for heart disease and stroke. It was unclear what level of this marker is cause for concern:

- Cleveland Clinic states borderline risk is between 14 – 30 mg/dL. High risk is 30-50. The highest risk is >50.
- Mount Sinai states normal is below 30.
- My local provider and the American Heart Association state that a value of > 50 may be an independent risk factor.

Considering all of that together, any value in the 14 – 50 range probably causes anxiety. But how can you be sure?

It's also important to note that various labs often use different test methods, which can result in different testing results and ranges. The unit of measurement might also vary between providers. The above test is a good example, with some labs using mg/dL and others using nmol/L.

Given all these variables, your best approach is to ask your physician for their perspective on interpreting your specific results.

ADDITIONAL SCREENING OPTIONS

The healthcare market is full of additional tests and tools you might find useful. Ask your provider for their perspective on the following.

- **Galleri blood test by GRAIL.** This multi-cancer measure detects up to 50 types of cancer and claims to identify the origin of the cancer with surprising accuracy. The test has high specificity, meaning it's unlikely to show a false positive (saying you have cancer, but you don't). The trade-off is the possibility of a false negative (you could have cancer, but the test doesn't pick it up). This tool is recommended for people aged 50 or older. Because standard blood tests generally can't detect cancer until the malignancy progresses significantly, I believe this test is worth considering. The biggest barrier is cost, currently $949, more than most people can afford.

- **Function Health.** Cofounded by Dr. Mark Hyman, this testing option provides truly comprehensive blood panels with over 100+ biomarkers. It's not cheap ($499 at last check), but it is another way to get a broad baseline on your health.

- **Prenuvo Whole Body Scans.** This is a cash-pay (out-of-pocket) MRI scan of your torso or complete body, ranging in cost from $999 to $2,499. I considered this test after my mom passed and before I had symptoms of my own. I didn't want a surprise like she experienced. One of my medical advisors cautioned against this scan, noting that the test would cause unnecessary anxiety by flagging a large percentage of people with non-issues, including false positives. At the time, I felt I was in amazing health and chose not to pursue it. Not surprisingly, I would now err on the side of knowing even if it had the potential to raise false positives that take time to sort through. Had I undergone this scan, doctors would have likely found my spot when it was Stage 1 and far more treatable than when it advanced to Stage 4.

SMART WATCHES/FITNESS MONITORS

Popular fitness trackers like the Apple Watch, Fitbit, Whoop, Oura or Garmin are useful for clarifying your baseline for several measures:

- **HRV (Heart Rate Variability).** HRV is the slight variations in time between heartbeats. The higher the HRV (the greater the variation), the better your general health. HRV is specific to each person and varies by age and gender, but understanding your baseline allows you to track meaningful changes down or up.

  Despite my high level of fitness prior to diagnosis, my HRV has always been relatively low, which perplexed me. I now realize my constant state of fight-or-flight gave little opportunity for my body to fully recover, putting my sympathetic nervous system in charge and suppressing my HRV. Any amount of alcohol also severely depresses overnight HRV, which can be a helpful reminder if you are trying to reduce your alcohol consumption over time.

- **Resting Heart Rate.** Your heart rate during sleep is another good measure of overall health. For people engaged in regular exercise, lower is better, but it can be a concern for others. This number can fluctuate day-to-day, potentially indicating stress and a need to recharge. Over a prolonged period, a change could suggest an investigation by your PCP. Overnight resting heart rate can dramatically increase with caffeine, alcohol, stress, or disrupted sleep.

- **Sleep Tracking.** Doctors and patients often debate the effectiveness of smartwatches and fitness monitors for measuring sleep, but many agree these tools can do well in raising awareness of general sleep trends, even if they wildly miss on measuring sleep stages. A friend who is a biomedical engineer with the US military notes that all these devices are fraught with inaccuracies but singles out the Oura device (a ring worn on your finger) as the best. The best resource on sleep and its importance for our wellbeing is Matthew Walker's book *Why We Sleep*.

BEHAVIORAL CHANGES

When I received my diagnosis, I made dramatic changes to my life. It's important to note that I had already made many small changes in the preceding years. For example, I have little trouble adhering to the diet and exercise that has helped in my healing, and I attribute that to unknowingly building the foundation prior to my diagnosis. Small changes made bigger changes possible.

Without those small successes, I'm not sure I would have been ready for further changes or if I would have stuck with them.

When I reached remission, multiple people told me, "Now the real work begins." Their meaning was that I needed to stay the course and keep up the habits I had built. My point? Wherever you are on your journey, start now and start small.

A perfect example comes from a past coworker who wanted to limit his dairy intake. He chose to swap out dairy creamer in his coffee for plant-based milks like soy or almond. Because he consumes multiple cups of coffee daily, this small change significantly reduced his intake not only of dairy but also of processed sugar. Compounded month over month and year over year, this tweak to his diet made a real difference.

Often, one small change leads to other small changes that become mutually reinforcing. Here are a few of the incremental changes I made before my diagnosis that set me up for good habits.

- **Eliminated soda.** I didn't just switch from regular to diet pop. Yep, I'm from the Midwest, where we call it "pop"! I worked to eliminate soda altogether. I customarily had a soda a day, typically in the afternoon when I felt low on energy. At work, I was trying to create a kidney care business that prioritized in-home dialysis. In the course of my research, I came across a study that found having two sodas a day created a two-fold risk of kidney disease compared to the group that didn't have any soda!.[3]

I didn't realize a daily decision like drinking soda could so significantly compromise my health. But I still needed an afternoon boost. I switched to coffee, but I needed cream and sugar to get it down. I drank coffee like this for a long time—until I was able to first skip the sugar and then the creamer. French vanilla creamer, I still miss you. I got by on black coffee until I realized it upset my stomach. I eventually landed on coffee with almond milk. The above progression happened over years, but it put me on a much better path.

- **Breath work.** I always thought, "You breathe how you breathe." It's automatic—nothing I could control and nothing to worry about. Although I started working on my breathing to improve my physical fitness, I learned that better breathing could alter my mood and mental state. I started to use Bas Rutten's O2 Trainer several days a week, usually after working out. It's a simple plastic device that restricts airflow. While it didn't improve my athletic ability, it prepared me for all the types of breathwork I would use as I learned various meditation techniques.

- **Took control of my phone.** Early smartphones were great at increasing productivity and connecting us with others. Now, however, they cause many of us to work more than ever. Scrolling through media and social media consumes more and more of our consciousness. I hit high alert when I noticed how frequently all four members of my family would occupy the same room yet be completely engrossed in their phones. I did the math and realized the four hours a day I spent on my phone meant I was giving away a quarter of my waking hours.

  Once I admitted my smartphone was outsmarting me, I took action to clean up my phone using steps by Tony Stubblebine.[4] The process required many steps and took multiple weeks to complete, but I reclaimed my phone. I can now use it with clear intention rather than fall under its control. And the result of being more present with others has been crucial to my healing journey.

Here's the truth. We all generally know what habits are healthy or unhealthy for us, but we often choose to stick with whatever feels easiest and most comfortable in the moment. Change is always hard, especially because changes for the sake of your long-term health can cause unpleasantness in the present.

But the results are worth it. I would encourage you to start small. Commit to just one change. See it through until it becomes a habit.

Once you master one new habit, commit to another change. Stack your progress. Ideally, your efforts will change overall health so you never get to the terrifying stage 4 reality I faced. However your own journey plays out, I guarantee you will be grateful for the changes you made. If you want an additional resource on this topic check out *Atomic Habits* by James Clear. They give you a stronger base from which to fight your cancer.

END NOTES

3 **National Center for Biotechnology Information (NCBI)**. *Carbonated Beverages and Chronic Kidney Disease*. Journal article. https://www.ncbi.nlm.nih.gov/pmc/articles/PMC3433753

4 **Better Humans (Medium).** *How to Set Up Your iPhone for Productivity, Focus, and Longevity.* Web article. https://betterhumans.pub/how-to-set-up-your-iphone-for-productivity-focus-and-your-own-longevity-bb27a68cc3d8

CHAPTER 21:

DIAGNOSIS

Although each journey with cancer is unique, at some point, every patient turns a corner from routine preventative healthcare to a focus on diagnosis—the need to rule in or out the possibility they might have cancer. They might be experiencing unusual symptoms, or their bloodwork looks suspicious, or their doctor cryptically states they need to undergo further testing.

KEY DIAGNOSTIC TESTS

Whatever triggers concerns about cancer, the first follow-up will likely be an ultrasound and/or an X-ray. These are crude tools compared to more sophisticated tests, but they can show the presence of something out of the ordinary.

If bloodwork or basic tests raise concerns, your doctor will almost certainly recommend one or more of four additional tests generally used to diagnose cancer and later assess ongoing progress.

It's important to understand the differences between each test so you can ask informed questions about which makes the most sense in your situation.

- **CT (Computerized Tomography) scan:** This series of X-rays examines the physical dimensions of solid tumors.[5] It's the fastest scan and generally preferable early on. There are a couple of noteworthy considerations:
  - **Dye.** A CT can be performed with or without dye. Injecting dye enhances the visibility of abnormalities but can be hard on your kidneys, so if you're at risk of kidney disease ask whether another test would be a better option. If you undergo a CT without dye, the radiologist who reads the scan will likely be cautious about providing a definitive diagnosis because the pictures were less than optimal. Because I was at risk of kidney damage, I opted for no dye. To my untrained eye, images with and without dye look very similar, so I was happy I pushed for this option.
  - **Cost.** While costs vary widely across providers, a CT scan is generally the most cost-effective diagnostic scan available.
- **MRI (magnetic resonance imaging) scan:** Unlike the CT scan, which uses X-rays, MRIs employ strong magnets and radio waves to generate images of the body.[6] Like a CT scan, this test will provide dimensions of the tumors. An MRI typically takes significantly longer (up to or over an hour compared to minutes for a CT scan) but renders a slightly more accurate picture. In some cancers, specifically brain and liver cancers, this is the preferred test. Other considerations to note:
  - **Claustrophobia.** If you're claustrophobic, you might want to opt for another test if possible. An MRI involves lying in a tube just a few inches from your face for a long time. Newer machines can be more spacious—even relatively open—with less whirring and clunky noise. A washcloth over your eyes might

be enough to make the experience tolerable. In some cases, your doctor can prescribe a mild sedative. Many clinics offer a choice of music as a distraction. But if you genuinely suffer in small spaces, your time in the tube can feel like forever. Talk it over with your doctor.

- **Dye.** Like a CT, an MRI can be done with or without injecting dye. Because this dye is believed to be less toxic to the kidneys, it felt like less of a worry for me.

- **Precision.** An MRI is more precise than other scans for judging changes in tumor size, so it's often the preferred post-treatment option to assess progress.

- **Cost.** An MRI is likely the most expensive of the four tests, a reason some insurance vendors won't approve the test.

• **PET (Positron Emission Tomography) Scan:** This test uses radioactive tracers with glucose to measure the metabolic activity of the tumors.[7] My lay-person perspective feels this test should be only used when other scans don't display the actual state of the cancer. This was my situation about eight months into treatment when the tumor dimensions hadn't changed, but we believed they were inactive. An MRI showed the tumors hadn't shrunk in size or number. The PET scan confirmed there was no metabolic activity and that I was in remission. Considerations:

- **Preparation.** There is significantly more preparation the day before (like changes in your diet) and the day of the test to ensure optimum results, such as sitting in a dark room for an hour prior to the test.

- **Dye.** Everyone has different comfort levels with radiation exposure for medical testing. Because the PET scan uses radioactive glucose, most people probably agree that fewer scans are better. Similarly, I try to minimize the intake of non-natural glucose whenever possible.

  - **Cost.** This test costs more than a CT scan. Depending on where it is performed, it could be comparable to an MRI.

- **Biopsy.** This minor surgery collects a tissue sample from a tumor. While other tests can be used at any point in the cancer journey, a biopsy typically only occurs early on as a means of confirming the diagnosis. Considerations:

  - **Surgery.** Any surgery has risk of complications, so while biopsies are typically minimally invasive, it's important to understand if there are alternatives that yield the certainty you need before proceeding with treatment.

  - **Cost.** Not surprisingly, a biopsy is the most expensive cost of the options.

As you move through your cancer journey, you will likely experience multiple of the above tests. I personally hit the grand slam—all of them in less than a year. It's important to understand why your doctor wants to use a specific test and to engage in an open discussion about what makes the most sense for your current state because in many cases the answer isn't clear-cut.

CERTAINTY OF DIAGNOSIS

For some types of cancer, the diagnosis is clear. Others require significant effort just to identify the specific cancer. For solid tumors, a biopsy is usually the best route to that answer. As they say, "tissue identifies the issue." That said, a recent study of prostate diagnoses found that an MRI was more accurate and less invasive than a biopsy.[8]

Most people get their initial diagnosis from a local oncologist, who is likely competent. However, it's unlikely that a person specializes in your type of cancer or conducts research to advance its treatment. For that reason, it can make sense to seek a second opinion at a center of excellence that has specific expertise in the suspected diagnosis.

A second opinion is your opportunity to get input from another oncologist or health system about your diagnosis or proposed treatment. If you choose this route, realize that one system's diagnosis will inevitably be questioned by other health systems.

REASONS TO SEEK SECOND OPINIONS

I believe there are specific situations when securing a second opinion from recognized experts can be helpful, if not highly recommended.

1. **Certainty of diagnosis.** Determining the presence and type of some cancers can be tricky. A biopsy generally provides conclusive evidence of cell type and cancer, but pathologists can still misread tissue samples. Asking another institution to evaluate sample slides can be advantageous. But this can be overdone. Even after my local hospital and two centers of excellence agreed on my diagnosis, another center wanted to reread the sample for themselves. It's unlikely insurance will cover more than a second opinion, giving you reason to push back because you do not want to be personally liable for a re-read of the sample.

2. **Certainty of treatment.** Chemo, then surgery? Surgery, then chemo? Radiation, then chemo? High dose chemo or low dose? Alternative/natural methods before undergoing chemo? Depending on your diagnosis, you might face a confusing set of choices, and sorting out these potential life-and-death decisions can create paralyzing fear.

   You likely want to start on your treatment path ASAP, but this isn't a choose-your-own-adventure book where you can flip back a page if your choice doesn't work out. You only get one shot at your best first treatment, meaning you might have good reason to obtain an expert second opinion on your best path forward before proceeding. Most malignancies grow slowly. If doctors believe that's the case for your cancer, you might decide you have time to get additional input. Disclaimer: I know someone who went to three centers of excellence and got three different treatment options. It made their treatment choice even harder.

3. **FOMO.** Fear of missing out is a common human reaction to life's issues, big and small. If you have the financial means and just want to be certain you're pursuing the best option to help you heal, you might choose to seek other help. Caution: I personally incurred a great financial and emotional cost for my center of excellence interactions. More pain than gain.

4. **Eligibility for clinical trials**. Some people believe that being a patient at a specific center of excellence gives them a better chance of being eligible for their clinical trials. However, the criteria for clinical trials is very specific, and most trials must actively search for patients. Personally, I wouldn't choose a center with that as my goal.

   A good starting point is searching for drug trials at clinicaltrials.gov. Temper your expectations that some meds prove effective while many others do nothing to increase life expectancy, so clinical trials are usually a last resort. Note: Most trials require you to stop any alternative/natural methods you might be using to boost your immune system or to heal. This helps ensure the integrity of studies but doesn't do patients any favors. One benefit of a clinical trial is that there is typically little to no cost to the patient for the actual treatment, although travel could be self-pay. It's another variable worth considering.

Second Opinion Data Logistics

Before you can see a doctor or even schedule a visit in some cases, the other facility will need to receive everything (such as medical records, scan images, and biopsy slides). Given the billions of Federal funding for healthcare interoperability, medical records transfer is generally less of an issue. But there still might be times when you need to download visit summaries or blood work and forward them to the facility.

A real issue can be getting your CT/MRI/PET scan images to

another center of excellence. Given their file size, these can't be simply emailed. You can wait for your oncologist's MA (medical assistant) to transfer the images, but then you're relying on their help while they are likely busy with other patients. Another option is to obtain a copy of the images yourself, typically a CD you can pick up. Before sending the physical CD to the facility, you can transfer electronically via a PowerShare account.[9] A few key points:

- Patients can indeed have PowerShare accounts. One center of excellence said this wasn't allowed and was shocked that we (the patient) transferred the images ourselves.
- Once you select the right facility name, you must select "share with" and select the right person's name. You will likely need to speak with someone at the facility to ensure you pick the right facility (they could have multiple sites) and the person's name (the name is generally not the physician you aim to see but someone else). If you don't select "share with," you might successfully transfer the files, but no one will be able to access them. This created a maddening loop for me where the recipient couldn't see the file nor delete them to let me try again.

After you send the files electronically, you could duplicate the CD and overnight the images to the facility if time is of the essence. We did this to reduce the risk of the center of excellence failing to receive the images and deciding to cancel our appointment.

AFFORDABLE ALTERNATIVES FOR SECOND OPINIONS

Unfortunately, the cost of accessing a distant or out-of-network center of excellence is often prohibitively expensive. Consider these alternatives:

1. **Get a second opinion from a local health system.** Nearly all insurance companies cover a second opinion. Check which local health systems are in-network and go to the other highest-rated system.

2. **Get a second opinion via remote consultation.** If you're already

working with the best local system and don't like other local options, your oncologist might be able to obtain a remote second opinion from a center of excellence. Companies such as Access Hope (oncology-specific) and RubiconMD (Broad specialties including oncology) could potentially assist. The site thesecondopinion.org offers a free second opinion for California residents. Follow up with both your oncologist and primary care provider to see if any of these are possibilities.

3. **Access nonprofits specializing in your cancer diagnosis.** If there is a nonprofit that focuses on your cancer, reaching out to them about standard treatments can confirm that you're following the recommended path. For GIST patients, the nonprofit is The Life Raft Group (liferaftgroup.org). For colorectal patients, there is the Colorectal Care Alliance (colorectalcancer.org).

4. **Join a peer group.** This is the least desirable option, but there is no shortage of groups on social media dedicated to specific cancers. While these groups provide a low-cost way to see what has or hasn't worked for other patients, the opinions offered likely come from non-experts. I personally found these groups incredibly depressing and avoided them to preserve my positive mental state.

SELECTING BETWEEN SOURCES OF SECOND OPINIONS

As you survey possible sources of expertise, consider these key factors:

- **In-network.** You can minimize personal financial risk by going to a system that's in-network. If you're unsure whether a health system is in-network, access your insurer's website or call your insurer for specifics.

- **Expertise.** While larger institutions like MD Anderson and Sloan Kettering are tremendous resources for almost all cancers, that doesn't guarantee they are the ultimate experts on your specific cancer, especially rare types. Support groups or nonprofits focused on your cancer can point you to the top centers of excellence and the best physicians. Although the University of Miami isn't traditionally considered a CoE, for example, I learned it has one of the foremost experts on GIST .

- **Distance.** How far are your top options? How you feel might make a flight or long drive impossible. Consider the fact that you might need to travel multiple times.

- **Mental health concerns.** Refer to the treatment section (page 177) for my discussion of preparing for these visits. If yours resemble mine, they will be emotionally draining.

- **Risks of hidden costs:** In preparation for your visit, the physician or system providing the second opinion will request all your imaging and visit information. As discussed above, a biopsy slide/sample will still need to be physically shipped. The system providing the second opinion will inevitably require tests to be rerun and slides to be reread. Make sure your insurance has pre-authorized these steps. One CoE put me on a recorded line to agree that I would cover the cost out of pocket if my insurance rejected coverage. I didn't realize I unwittingly approved a nearly $100K personal liability. Don't do this! Demand that the provider work with your insurance so you know if additional testing is covered before the expense is incurred.

Certainty of diagnosis is critical. If you begin a treatment plan and later discover it targeted the wrong diagnosis, you have lost precious time. For this reason, I think it's generally worth the effort and expense of getting a second opinion. The process also grants you peace of mind that no errors have occurred in your life-or-death case.

HEARING THE DIAGNOSIS

Hearing "you have cancer" is deeply profound. Even if you're later completely healed and there is no evidence of disease (NED), you're forever changed. As I described earlier, I was numb for the first few days. Soon after, negative thoughts invaded my brain to the point that they jolted me awake every morning. While I will defer to experts on how to appropriately process a diagnosis and the layers of grief it creates, I learned during my journey that I could redirect my thoughts and say, "I'm not thinking about that today. I'm going to think about this instead." Such a simple technique might sound ridiculous, but prior to my diagnosis I let my brain roam wherever it wanted. Whatever it wanted to think, I let it think.

I don't intend this technique as a way to ignore or suppress emotions. I realized, however, that my brain was so accustomed to stress that whenever life and work were sailing along quite well, my mind seized the opportunity to make up stressful situations just to get a cortisol fix. It took me a while to admit I was addicted to my own stress hormones and then train myself to not let my brain run wild.

As the Stoic philosopher Seneca wrote in his 13th letter, "We suffer more often in imagination than reality."

In the wake of the diagnosis, banishing these negative invaders was critical to getting my mindset in the right place to start my healing journey.

One of my first actions post-diagnosis was to write sticky tabs messages I wanted to see every morning. "Attitude is Everything." "You've got this." "Best thing that happened today." Within hours of learning I had cancer, I began posting these notes on my bathroom mirror to ensure they were the first thing I read every morning. Over time, this "manifestation mirror" expanded with pictures, Bible verses, cards from friends, love notes from my wife, and even a handwritten note from basketball announcer Dick Vitale! I can't think of a better way to start the day than to direct my mind. It was my note to self: THIS IS WHAT WE'RE GOING TO THINK ABOUT TODAY.

REACH OUT TO EAP

Your Employee Assistance Program (EAP) is likely the best health benefit you didn't know you had.

Most health plans provide some form of EAP benefit. In the wake of your diagnosis—exactly when you urgently need to talk to someone NOW—your EAP service can be a great help. Many cities and rural areas suffer from a severe shortage of mental health professionals, and the first available appointment might be weeks or months away. People on call at an EAP phoneline or video call exist at this moment. They are professionals available to talk with you during a crisis as well as refer you to a local therapist. Cancer doesn't wait, and EAP can provide rapid access to the help you need to process your emotions.

Note that most EAP plans also provide a wealth of other services rarely utilized. I tapped the service to locate a great nursing home for my grandma. A coworker accessed EAP to help plan a family Disney World vacation. Other services typically include financial and legal services, family planning and childcare, eldercare assistance, and educational programs. While many of these offerings might feel less relevant at the moment of diagnosis, they offer help with important concerns that might otherwise fall through the cracks as you deal with your illness.

LIBER8

In many cases, an emotional root cause is tied to the cancer diagnosis. As I discussed in telling my story, I met with several talk therapists, peer counselors, faith-based counselors, and more. While these were all helpful in their own way, I never felt we were getting to the actual root of the issue. At my wife's recommendation, I tried Liber8 (liber8.health), an online tool paired with a 90-minute emotional mapping session. My hour and a half with a complete stranger brought up memories I had completely forgotten, which helped me understand why I might have cancer. Now, I might not have had this breakthrough without all the other work I had already done, but I raise it here as a unique resource that might help if you aren't making progress using traditional approaches.

UNDERSTAND YOUR HEALTH COVERAGE

As you start to navigate a variety of tests and appointments, it's critical that you get to know your health insurance, especially what is and isn't covered.

First, if you haven't already done so, ensure you can log on to the insurer's portal to get real-time information on medical claims and the provider's network status. Key items to be aware of:

- **Insurance company.** Assuming you have medical coverage, this is the organization that administers your medical insurance. The terms "health plan," "payer," or "payor" refer to the same entity.

- **Provider:** This overarching term refers to anyone delivering clinical care, including a hospital, medical group, outpatient facility, etc.

- **Type of plan.**

  - **HMO** stands for **Health Management Organization.** In an HMO, you either select your PCP or one is assigned to you. While HMO plans are typically more affordable, they also require you to see your PCP before you can see any specialist. In this scenario, it's critical to get an appointment as soon as possible, because that professional likely controls your access to the right specialists.

  - **PPO** stands for **Preferred Provider Organization,** and in these plans, you generally don't need your PCP's referral to schedule an appointment with a specialist. You still need to figure out which specialist you want to see.

- What providers and health systems are **in network**?
  - Again, logging onto the insurer's portal and confirming a physician is in the network is critical to reducing or limiting the ultimate cost to you.
- Choosing **good providers.**
  - Most health plans have a "premium" designation for providers that meet specific quality metrics for the health plan. If you have nothing else to go on, start there. Many of these designations aren't based on substantial data, and few consider bedside manner, which I believe is one of the most important considerations when choosing an oncologist.
- **Financial terms** of your insurance.
  - **Out-of-pocket maximum.** If you have a family, there are typically four out-of-pocket maximum numbers, two if not.
    - **In-network Individual:** The most expense one person can incur during a plan year (if seeing an in-network provider). Most but not all plans are on calendar years, but confirm the dates for your plan.
    - **In-network Family:** The most expense a family in total can incur during a plan year. It's quite likely the family member with the diagnosis will meet their out-of-pocket maximum, but that doesn't necessarily mean other family members won't incur costs unless the family maximum has been met.
    - **Out-of-network Individual:** The most one person can incur if they use providers who aren't in-network. This is typically significantly larger, with the maximum exceeding over $100K in some cases. This underlines the necessity to stay in-network whenever possible.
    - **Out-of-network Family:** The most expense a family in total can incur during a plan year, but with a much higher number.

- **Deductibles.** Although you and your employer pay monthly premiums for your healthcare coverage, as you start incurring healthcare expenses, you typically must pay the full amount for specialist or hospital visits until you meet a designated amount, the "deductible."

  As with the out-of-pocket maximum, there are deductible amounts for the four categories described above. Once you meet the deductible, the plan typically pays a certain percentage of a bill (such as 80%) and you pay the remainder until you reach the out-of-pocket maximum.

  Most plans allow and encourage at least one visit per plan year with your PCP at no additional cost, another reason to know and go to your PCP before a serious medical condition occurs.

- **Co-pays**. Co-pays are what many providers charge per visit, sometimes demanding it when you check-in. The co-pay amounts vary. Specialist and emergency room visits are typically higher compared to primary care and outpatient visits.

  Importantly, if you believe you have met your out-of-pocket maximum, you can decline to pay the co-pay at check-in. You can cite that reason and ask the provider to dispute the claim. If you don't, getting your $20 or $50 payment reimbursed can be very time-consuming. It's a hassle you don't need when you're trying to heal yourself.

- **Balance billing.** This is when a provider bills you the difference between what they charge and what insurance covers. When you go out of network, this is a frequent occurrence, which is yet another major reason to stay in-network where possible.

  Note that even providers who are in-network sometimes bill you directly. If you have a co-pay due for a visit, it's crucial to know that amount is your ENTIRE financial responsibility for that visit, and the provider cannot balance bill you for the difference. This happened to me with my mental health provider. I should have been charged $20 per visit, but I was balance-billed over $200 per visit. The front desk person tried to get me to pay that amount at the time of check-in. You can and should decline if you don't understand why you're being charged a specific amount.

- **PHI: Personal Health Information.** This is any information in the medical record or designated record set that can be used to identify an individual and that was created, used, or disclosed in the course of providing a health care service such as diagnosis or treatment.[10]

- **HIPAA: Health Insurance Portability and Accountability Act.** This federal law was passed in 1996 to protect patients' health information. It generally prohibits healthcare providers and businesses called "covered entities" from disclosing protected information to anyone other than a patient and the patient's authorized representatives without their consent.[11]

  It's vital to note that you have the right to view your own medical records from a provider. Typically these are available in a patient portal. I will note that a good friend of mine was forbidden from seeing their medical chart with the provider, who cited HIPAA. Outside of psychotherapy notes, you're ALWAYS allowed to see your medical records. In this instance, the provider was creating fraudulent chart notes to justify unnecessary surgeries. If this ever happens to you, it's either a gross error or a red flag that a provider is potentially up to something nefarious.

UNDERSTANDING PRIOR AUTHORIZATIONS

Prior authorizations are a point of exasperation for me and many cancer and non-cancer patients alike. Given the potential delays this process can cause to your receiving treatment, it's critical that you understand how to push a "prior auth" or "PA" forward.

- **What is "prior authorization"?**
  Depending on the test or drug you need, your insurance company might require someone to approve it before they agree to cover the cost. If you proceed with a test without getting authorization, you could be liable for the entire cost of the procedure, which can be a debilitating dollar amount.

- **Why do insurance companies insist on prior authorizations?**
  Prior authorizations are intended to save money by reducing medical expenses the insurer believes are unnecessary as well as to limit fraudulent or low-value tests. However, this additional layer of approval has angered patients and physicians alike. UnitedHealth Group vowed to cut nearly 20% of their prior authorizations.[12] The Kaiser Foundation noted, however, that there were over 35 million prior authorizations in 2021 for Medicare Advantage plans.[13] Even with a 20% reduction, each of the 27 million Americans enrolled in a Medicare Advantage plan in 2021[14] would still need to deal with at least one prior authorization per year. It should be noted that there have been progressive discussions about insurers lessening the number of prior authorizations yet you are still quite likely to encounter them.

- **What's the best way to navigate prior authorizations?**
  Prior authorization typically happens behind the scenes when the hospital or medical group submits orders for a test. The order is sent to the insurance company's prior authorization department, where their medical management teams review the order for appropriateness. If there are any questions, they will contact the provider and then approve or reject the orders.

  This process typically happens electronically and can take multiple days to complete. IMPORTANT: If getting the test is time-sensitive, the insurance company typically has a phone number the provider can call to escalate the review. I had to do this, and I eventually brought together a three-way call to ensure the right people from the insurance company and provider talked to each other. Don't be afraid to confirm the prior authorization has been completed and push for a phone call to resolve if needed.

While prior authorization typically occurs behind the scenes, a cancer center of excellence told me it was my responsibility to ensure the prior authorization for an MRI was completed, meaning that if the insurance company didn't cover the test, it was my fault, not theirs. While I find this ridiculous when you and your family are trying to get the care you need, don't be surprised if this burden gets pushed to you. I recommend speaking with the prior authorization department at the hospital or medical group and obtaining confirmation that they have received the approval. If they haven't, then I recommend setting up a three-way call as I did above to ensure the approval gets resolved.

In the end, you should receive a prior authorization number or other code that can be referenced in the insurance company's system in the event there is an issue. Don't throw away or delete this information.

If you receive your insurance through your employer, another avenue is asking your Human Resources department for contacts with the insurer who can help navigate the prior authorization process.

Once you're further along in your journey, it's quite likely a Care Manager from the insurance company will be assigned to your case. While quality varies wildly, this person is another potential resource to help resolve any administrative issues you encounter.

SELECTING AN ONCOLOGIST

At the request of a friend, I spoke to a woman whose mom had recently been diagnosed with pancreatic cancer. Unfortunately, the cancer was discovered during a visit to the emergency department. The oncologist on-call by default became her ongoing oncologist for treatment. While the mom and her family didn't like the oncologist, they didn't realize they could switch.

Ideally, you will develop a deep relationship with your oncologist who will work with you for many years. Don't simply accept an oncologist you're referred or assigned to. While it can seem like a tremendous burden to find the right oncologist, I strongly believe it's worth the effort. The further you proceed in your treatment plan, the more a new oncologist will need time to get up to speed.

You need to trust this human with life decisions, so if their bedside manner hits you wrong, it's time to find another one. Most oncologists are part of a larger group, so ideally you can interview other oncologists within that group and switch. Meeting with other oncologists will likely require additional phone calls or referrals, but if you are planning for success, I believe it is worth the effort.

BRINGING AN ALLY TO YOUR APPOINTMENTS

There is an old saying: "God gave us two ears and one mouth so we can listen twice as much as speak." In the case of healthcare, remember that "Four ears are better than two." This is especially true when you meet with a doctor. Little-known fact: There are roughly 170,000 words in the English language, and Taber's Medical Cyclopedic Medical Dictionary notes that approximately 55,000 are medical terms.[15] The fact that many of us know only a tiny fraction of those terms is reason enough to have notepad and ears ready.

I always recommend having someone attend any critical appointment with you. Depending on the topic, appointments can be highly emotional, which makes it even harder to understand what is being discussed and recommended. It's important for both of you to take notes to compare at the end of the appointment or immediately afterward. I know firsthand from attending a few of my mom's appointments that interpretations can vary widely by family member. If this isn't possible, ask if you can record the conversation and/or have your AI assistant listen to the appointment to summarize the key points for you.

CONTROLLING INFORMATION OVERLOAD

Your first instinct upon getting news of a diagnosis is to start searching online for anything you can find about your cancer. I can't put into words how STRONGLY I recommend against this. I made my dad swear to me that he would stop googling my cancer because, inevitably, I knew from his demeanor or questions when he found something very negative. Yes, you need to rapidly get up to speed, but there's absolutely a right way and wrong way to do this.

Who should search? In some cases, you don't have a choice. It will have to be you. I was fortunate that my wife was able and willing to do most of the research for me so I could stay in a positive mindset. You can be incredibly careful in your search and still stumble on information and comments that are negative and unhelpful. Asking a family member or friend to take the lead on this goes a long way to maintaining your mental outlook.

Where to search? Once you type your search term into a search engine, thousands of links pop up. Even within the most relevant links, it makes sense to proceed with caution. Please skip the Reddit feeds, which rarely go anywhere good. I recommend restricting your search primarily to the following:

- **Academic Centers of Excellence.** Institutions such as MD Anderson, Cleveland Clinic, Dana-Farber, Memorial Sloan Kettering, Cedars Sinai, Mayo Clinic, City of Hope, Yale Medicine, and Duke Medicine are all world-renowned as cancer centers of excellence.

- **National and government sites.** Institutions including the American Cancer Society, National Cancer Institute, and National Institute of Health (NIH) are among the best. National sites of other countries are also potentially good resources.

- **Wikipedia.** If you want a good summary of your cancer, this online group-sourced encyclopedia can be a helpful start. The benefit? Entries provide links to sources, papers, and publications that can prove useful. You will also find external links with information more specific to your cancer than some sites listed above. Important note: The Wikipedia page for my cancer had images not for the faint of heart.

- **PubMed.** This is a virtual one-stop resource for published research and clinical trials about your cancer. It "comprises more than 37 million citations for biomedical literature from MEDLINE, life science journals, and online books." As such, the site can be incredibly confusing for non-medical readers. I recommend the Good vs. Bad Science podcast by Bob Kaplan and Dr. Peter Attica to understand how to properly read and understand these studies.[16]

- **Social Media.** While I personally avoid social media, I realize that other cancer survivors disagree with me. Despite the rarity of my cancer, I quickly found multiple national and international groups to join. My brief visits weren't helpful. The sites were full of desperate pleas and death, topics I didn't want to impact my mindset. However, these sites could prove helpful in finding organizations and non-profits dedicated to your cancer diagnosis, which can be essential resources for locating expert practitioners and the latest clinical trials.

FOCUS ON YOUR DIAGNOSIS—NOT YOUR PROGNOSIS

I found that many authors and survivors agree with this sentiment:

Don't spend your days pondering your prognosis. Focus first on your diagnosis, then on treatment options.

I noted earlier that I intentionally didn't want to know the five-year survival rate for my cancer. In fact, almost two years later, I still don't know it. Why? I didn't want to limit my thinking of what was possible. After all, prognosis is a spectrum—a range of averages—and each of us is a unique human.

I love my local oncologist. During a particularly rough patch, he said, "You need to plan for a good outcome and live that way. Always waiting for the other shoe to drop is no way to live." This was particularly helpful advice. Others might argue we need a more realistic assessment. But every person is different. The severity of every case varies. And I know the power of the mind. If you don't create some possibility in the mind of the upside, then there is no way it will happen. No one knows how long they have, and most believe they have more time than they likely do. So live in the moment and savor it.

END NOTES

5 **Wikipedia.** *Computed Tomography (CT) Scan.* Reference article. https://en.wikipedia.org/wiki/CT_scan\

6 **Wikipedia.** *Magnetic Resonance Imaging (MRI).* Reference article. https://en.wikipedia.org/wiki/Magnetic_resonance_imaging

7 **Wikipedia.** *Positron Emission Tomography (PET).* Reference article. https://en.wikipedia.org/wiki/Positron_emission_tomography

8 **Healthline.** *When Looking for Prostate Cancer, Which Is Best, MRI or Biopsy?* Medical overview article. https://www.healthline.com/health/prostate-cancer/prostate-mri-vs-biopsy

9 **Nuance PowerShare.** *Secure Medical Image Sharing Platform.* Healthcare technology service. https://www1.nuancepowershare.com/smr/registration/signup.action

10 **University of California, Berkeley – Committee for Protection of Human Subjects (CPHS).** *HIPAA PHI: Definition of PHI and List of 18 Identifiers.* Regulatory guidance. https://cphs.berkeley.edu/hipaa/hipaa18.html

11 **Wikipedia.** *Health Insurance Portability and Accountability Act (HIPAA).* Reference article. https://en.wikipedia.org/wiki/Health_Insurance_Portability_and_Accountability_Act

12 **Fierce Healthcare.** *UnitedHealthcare to Begin Reducing Prior Authorizations.* Healthcare industry news. https://www.fiercehealthcare.com/payers/unitedhealthcare-begin-reducing-prior-authorizations-summer

13 **Kaiser Family Foundation (KFF).** *Medicare Advantage Insurers Made Nearly 50 Million Prior Authorization Determinations in 2023.* Issue brief, republished Jan 28, 2025. https://www.kff.org/medicare/issue-brief/over-35-million-prior-authorization-requests-were-submitted-to-medicare-advantage-plans-in-2021/

14 **America's Health Insurance Plans (AHIP).** *Medicare Advantage Demographics.* Industry report (PDF). https://ahiporg-production.s3.amazonaws.com/documents/202312-AHIP_MA-Demographics-Report-v05.pdf

15 **Eton Institute.** *How Many Words Are in the English Language (95/5 RULE)?* Educational article. https://www.linkedin.com/pulse/how-many-words-english-language-955-rule-etoninstitute

16 **Peter Attia, MD.** *Good vs. Bad Science: How to Read and Understand Scientific Studies.* Podcast / educational article. https://peterattiamd.com/how-to-read-and-understand-scientific-studies/

CHAPTER 22:
TREATMENT

After working through the difficult steps of testing and diagnosis, most people dealing with cancer feel some degree of relief as they begin treatment. But this part of the journey brings its own challenges, which might include feeling physically worse before you feel better. This section helps you navigate treatment and stay as whole as possible in body, mind, and soul.

There's no one-size-fits-all treatment for cancer. As with the first diagnosis, some types have only one course of action. Other cancers present multiple treatment options.

UNDERSTANDING TREATMENT OPTIONS

As you plot a course forward, your oncologist will work with you to understand your options for treatment.

- **Identify potential options.** While your oncologist will be well-versed in standard protocols, few are aware of every new treatment option or drugs undergoing clinical trials. Knowing everything is beyond reach. Most oncologists treat a wide range of cancers, and there's so much research going on that it's impossible to stay abreast of every advancement.

Even centers of excellence don't know everything. Each clinic focuses on its own trials as opposed to those conducted by others. You can search via clinicaltrials.gov for all current trials in the United States. In addition, social media groups and nonprofit organizations dedicated to your cancer ideally will track all the potential trials, their criteria for admission, and whether they're accepting new patients. If you find a trial that seems like a fit, don't hesitate to bring it up with your oncologist.

- **Determine effectiveness.** It's not enough for treatments to exist. You want to know how well they work. Key things to understand: How many people have undergone a particular treatment? Are those people like you—age, gender, race, cancer stage? How have people responded to treatment? For reference, there was only one study of my mom's medication, which occurred in South Korea, and fewer than 100 humans took part. The small test size and specific peer group weren't great indicators of how my European mom would likely respond to the treatment.

- **Consider side-effects.** All drugs have side-effects, and some can be severe. It's therefore critical to understand the full range of frequency and severity. One note of caution: For almost any drug, the side effects will be a laundry list of potential reactions. In the case of my medication, I kept myself deliberately unaware of side effects beyond the three most common. I didn't want to obsess over negative possibilities, and I worried that my mind would imagine or even create bad outcomes. My approach might sound extreme, but keeping my mind in the right mental state was essential, and Jing was on watch for all the rest.

- **Non-traditional treatment options.** The more you research treatments and talk to patients, the more you will hear of potential treatments that likely sound crazy at first, like getting a daily coffee enema. Yep, that's a thing! I have accumulated a long list of what some would consider "woo woo" options. Just as with traditional treatments, you need to understand potential side effects, how to measure if a treatment is working for you, and if there are any contraindications with your traditional treatment. Some of the more common non-traditional treatment options follow. Please do your own research before pursuing any of these:

- **Acupuncture.** I personally no longer consider this approach non-traditional, but I recognize many people still quiver at the thought of getting poked with needles. Acupuncture helps move your energy ("chi") to ensure it doesn't get stuck or to help it get unstuck. A skilled acupuncturist can focus on lessening pain, improving energy, improving digestion, and preparing for chemotherapy or surgery.

- **IV Vitamin C.** This everyday vitamin is known to be toxic to cancer cells, so the belief is that getting enough vitamin C can contribute to killing cancer cells. It's been proven that taking vitamin C via pill isn't effective. Yet, it's believed that vitamin C can reach a therapeutic level via IV. IV treatments are expensive and time-consuming (more than $200 an hour per session). Advocates recommend one or two IVs per week, so sustaining this approach quickly becomes a challenge. The Riordan Clinic in Kansas is a major proponent of this treatment. Note the earlier disclaimer regarding additional G6PD level testing if you have low hemoglobin.

- **Mistletoe therapy.** Injecting liquid mistletoe is said to create an immune response that strengthens the body's ability to fight cancer growth.

- **Ozone (IV, Eboo, or rectal).** Like vitamin C, ozone is toxic to cancer cells. Getting the ozone to the tumor could make it additive in the fight. In the past, it's been difficult to get enough ozone into your system to reasonably believe some of it would reach the tumor. The Eboo (Extracorporeal Blood Oxygenation and Ozonation) machine can now infuse a few liters of blood with ozone, increasing the chance that some ozone makes it to the tumor. Logically, rectal ozone makes sense for colon or colorectal cancer.

- **Hyperbaric oxygen.** Cancer cells create low-oxygen environments in which to grow, so proponents assert that hyperbaric oxygen floods the system with oxygen and disrupts cancer growth. I met a survivor with a rare jaw cancer who credits this treatment with saving his life. The question of what level of chamber is necessary to achieve a therapeutic level is hotly debated.

Each of the above approaches has some basis in science and logic, but because none involves an expensive pharmaceutical or technology, there are limited studies assessing actual effectiveness. And again, just like with any traditional treatment, you need to weigh efficacy, cost, time, and possible side effects before proceeding.

In all practicality, you might not have much choice or any choice about the Western medicine treatment you pursue. There might be only one option, or your oncologist might strongly advocate for one approach. Whatever the case, it becomes crucial to actively manage your experience of treatment and consider what, if any, non-traditional treatment options make sense.

MANAGING TREATMENT

Depending on your diagnosis and treatment plan, it's likely you will undergo some combination of chemotherapy, radiation, and surgery. Each approach can have a variety of impacts on your body that you will need to manage.

MITIGATING SIDE EFFECTS

As hinted above, you want to be aware of a drug's primary side effects while inviting an ally to study up on lesser-known effects. It's simply a load you don't need to carry unless a side-effect presents itself. It can be helpful to track your side effects and identify potential triggers that worsen your symptoms, and I found the phone app Wave Health: Symptom Tracker useful.

Some research supports that fasting while receiving chemotherapy can minimize nausea and other side effects.[17] Fred Evard, author of *How My Immune System Beat Cancer*, purposely experimented on himself. He fasted for his first chemotherapy treatment and felt fine. The next time he received chemotherapy, he ate as usual and found he experienced nausea and significant pain. Fasting isn't always advisable, so ask your oncologist.

GETTING SUPPORT

Once you're diagnosed, your health plan will likely assign a case manager to partner with you to coordinate care and navigate administrative frustrations such as prior authorizations. Not everyone will find this support helpful, but it's worth meeting your care manager to assess that person's skills and fit. You might discover another helpful member of your cancer-fighting team.

ONGOING TREATMENT OPTIONS

Ideally, your initial treatment is the only treatment you need to reach remission and NED (no evidence of disease). If the first treatment doesn't get you to your desired goal, be aware of other options that might exist. Revisit the clinical trial sources above to determine what else you should consider.

PREPARING YOUR BODY FOR TREATMENT

As a family, we did extensive research to optimize my body's response to treatment. Again, I'm not a doctor. But I found these items helpful.

GLUCOSE

For me, when it comes to diet, the elephant in the room is glucose and its relationship with cancer cells.

- In 1922, Otto Warburg published a study demonstrating that cancer cells consume glucose at a far higher rate than normal cells, a discovery that became known as the Warburg Effect (en.wikipedia.org).

- This finding has caused many to speculate that starving the body of glucose could potentially starve cancer cells.

- Most individuals consume huge amounts of glucose via refined and non-refined sugars. In 1800, Americans ate an average of seven pounds of sugar per year. Today we ingest more than 100 pounds of sugar per year! (www.cell.com).

- The average American weighs 181 pounds (men 200, women 162), a metric that has increased 20 pounds just since 1990 (news.gallup.com). That means we eat more than 55% of our body weight in sugar each year. Staggering!

While most health institutions acknowledge that high sugar consumption is a primary cause of today's obesity epidemic, they don't promote the idea that reducing sugar could help fight cancer. Although no study shows this approach to be effective, I also can't find research that shows limiting sugar isn't effective.

This lack of data means few healthcare providers will advise you to cut your sugar intake. In fact, many do the opposite. My mom, for example, was encouraged to eat whatever she wanted, including ice cream. I recognize that a patient having difficulty ingesting calories needs to get fuel however they can. But for many patients, limiting processed sugar seems wise. Note that your body and brain do need glucose to function, so the answer isn't the extreme of quitting all foods your body naturally converts to glucose.

In short, I concluded that if glucose is a primary food source of cancer cells, I can't see how consuming less glucose would harm me. At worst, the improvement in overall health and weight control makes my body better able to fight cancer. Other than missing the taste of a nice pastry or a cookie fresh out of the oven, I didn't see much downside. I would happily give up sugary treats to see my children grow up.

I still consume natural sugar through fruits, but we quickly removed almost all processed sugar. This effort did require constant monitoring. Restarting travel for work meant being faced with new foods, and almost any packaged food contains added sugar, even whole wheat buns and brown rice (which caused us to switch to Ezekiel bread). I don't worry about naturally occurring sugar. My focus is on minimizing added sugar. As I evolved my diet, I eventually cut out all grains, which are quickly converted to glucose and can cause spikes. I did feel lethargic for a time, but I also gained the additional benefit of eliminating my exposure to GMO grains and grain-borne pesticides.

CGM (Continuous Glucose Monitor)

If you know someone with diabetes, they likely wear a continuous glucose monitor. It's a far better option than pricking a finger throughout the day to check glucose levels. Instead, the user inserts a sensor under the skin, which sends a continual reading of glucose levels to their cellphone. This technology has advanced significantly, making devices less painful to apply and measurements more accurate.

So what does a CGM have to do with cancer? To minimize glucose spikes, you need to know what causes them. While donuts and soda obviously flood your system with excess glucose, a CGM uncovers less obvious culprits so you can fine-tune your diet.

The foods that cause glucose spikes are highly specific to each human being, and the CGM is a personalized, real-time tracker.

Wearing a CGM for a month or two gives you a sense of what to avoid, and the results can be surprising. In my case, eating cold oats in the afternoon caused a spike, but adding a dill pickle prevented spikes. And while my wife's glucose spikes from a bowl of breakfast oatmeal, mine doesn't even blip. Note: Don't be surprised if your glucose spikes immediately after working out. It's a normal process as your body produces glucose for ready energy.

In his book *Outlive*, Peter Attia says everyone should wear a CGM to better understand this important process. I can't grasp why every oncologist doesn't prescribe a CGM to patients newly diagnosed with cancer. It's even more baffling that the healthcare world doesn't support this kind of personalized discovery. Over-the-counter CGMs are readily available, but Jing and I requested prescriptions from our PCPs. Ironically, I needed prior authorization to obtain a device that would help me understand my glucose, lose weight, decrease my chance of getting type 2 diabetes, and potentially drastically improve the outcome of my cancer journey. To get a device without prior auth, I would need to have been diagnosed with painful and expensive chronic diabetes. CGMs are a tiny investment in improving long-term health and reducing healthcare costs system-wide.

SUPERCHARGING YOUR DIET

The topic of diet is so charged that most doctors never talk with patients about what and how much they eat. Because no one was eager to offer food advice for dealing with cancer, Jing and I waded headfirst into the jungle. What we share below is our non-expert understanding of the data, logic, and results of various approaches. As always, take what you want from our input and forget the rest.

What you eat or don't eat isn't

a "set it and forget it" thing.
As your condition changes,
so should your approach to diet.

There are many books completely dedicated to discussing food and cancer. A few we found particularly helpful were:

- *Radical Remission: Surviving Cancer Against All Odds* by Kelly A. Turner
- *How to Starve Cancer* by Jane McLelland
- *Good Energy* by Dr. Casey Means with Calley Means
- Nutritionfacts.org is a nonprofit founded by Michael Greger, M.D. FACLM. This website provides free updates on the latest nutrition research presented in bite-sized videos, blogs, podcasts, and infographics. If you want the latest research in an easily digestible format—Dad pun intended—start here.

We were also greatly assisted by a naturopathic doctor. Be aware that the assessment of "naturopath" by Wikipedia and other online sources can be scathing, saying practitioners employ methods based on "vitalism and folk medicine rather than evidence-based medicine" and the practice has been characterized as "quackery".[18] While some of my naturopath's practices seemed a bit "woo woo," his multiple-page intake form and 90-minute initial visit convinced me he was serious about understanding me thoroughly, and his approach to food made intuitive sense to me.

The doctor proposed two diets that can help in healing our body from cancer and presented a third as healthful but neutral in regard to cancer:

1. **Ketosis.** This isn't the diet where you eat all the meat you want, which is what many people mean when they say they "did keto." Ketosis focuses on consuming healthy fats and eliminating almost all carbohydrates which switches your body from using glucose to ketones as its primary energy source.

   Why? Cancer cells can't process ketones, so this approach starves them of their primary ingredient for survival. The challenge is getting into and staying in ketosis, which requires daily monitoring of your ketone levels using urine test strips. You need to stay in ketosis without entering ketoacidosis, a state that requires immediate medical attention. The naturopath has patients who have maintained ketosis for multiple years.

2. **Plant-based vegan.** This approach eliminates all animal products and almost all processed foods. While you still utilize glucose for energy, you effectively eliminate all processed sugar and only ingest glucose that naturally occurs in fruits and vegetables.

   While Western medicine argues that no research to date proves this diet works in fighting cancer, the books listed above offer multiple people with dramatic success following this approach. While these stories didn't occur in controlled studies, they provide a large enough sample size to give hope—and when death looms far faster than you ever imagined, hope might be all you need.

3. **Mediterranean Diet.** This popular diet focuses on vegetables, unprocessed carbohydrates, legumes, and fish, with some olive oil on top. The naturopath felt this diet doesn't fight cancer, but it also doesn't feed cancer growth.

I was ready to do anything I could to heal my body. The naturopath didn't advocate for one diet over the others but simply laid out options and trade-offs. Because I doubted my ability to get my body into ketosis and stay there, going vegan was the obvious choice for me.

While many other diets exist, these options offer broad alternatives for thinking about cancer and diet. In my research with Jing, I concluded that believing a particular diet is working for you is probably reason enough to stick with it. We know little about the power of the mind, and I defer to your ability to discern the connections between what you ingest and the results you experience.

Another naturopath we met did an interesting test. She instructed me to extend my arm, then placed a vial of a single food on my body. All the vials looked the same, so I had no idea what was in them. She then asked me to keep my arm strong while she pushed down. Most of the time, I held my arm up, but in a few instances my arm gave way. Skeptical about what was happening, I switched arms, closed my eyes, and tried multiple times to keep my arm strong. Jing laughed at my attempts to keep my arm horizontal just to watch it bounce down as pressure was applied. Some of the results were shocking. Based on this test, I should avoid chickpeas (and hummus), grains, and most beans. The feedback helped me further evolve my diet to something that made sense to me. There are other food "sensitivity" tests available but upon researching them I could not find one that was credible and gave consistent results, so I don't have any to recommend at this time.

FOODS TO POTENTIALLY AVOID

Several everyday foods have carcinogenic links, and others have potential positive impacts on healing your body. I highlight the most common foods to avoid or emphasize.

- **Dairy.** The protein casein that naturally occurs in dairy is believed to be carcinogenic. A meta-analysis in PubMed involving 700,000 people found that increased consumption of whole milk by males led to an increased mortality risk of prostate cancer but didn't find significant cancer linkages to consumption of other dairy products, including milk, yogurt, cheese, or butter.[19]

  An additional consideration: Much of our dairy comes from livestock injected with hormones, with at best uncertain effects on human health.

- **Red meat:** A meta-analysis in PubMed reviewed 148 published articles on the connection between cancer and consumption of unprocessed red meat, processed red meat, and total red meat. The results weren't encouraging for lovers of red meat:

  1. **Higher consumption of unprocessed red meat** led to statistically higher rates of breast cancer, endometrial cancer,

colorectal cancer, colon cancer, rectal cancer, lung cancer, and hepatocellular carcinoma.

2. **Higher consumption of processed red meat** led to a 6% greater risk of breast cancer, 18% greater risk of colorectal cancer, 21% colon cancer risk, 22% rectal cancer risk, and 12% greater lung cancer risk.

3. **Higher consumption of all red meat** correlated with statistically higher rates of colorectal, colon, rectal, lung and renal cancers.[20]

What's the connection between red meat and cancer? The short answer is that the ample heme iron (iron from animal sources) in red meat triggers significant inflammation in the body, which is believed to be a precursor to cancer cell development. A more precise explanation can be found in this article.[20]

- **Alcohol.** I love alcohol. More accurately, I used to love alcohol. Although I truly miss sipping tequila, alcohol poisons our bodies. The most recent research concurs that no amount is safe to consume. An MD Anderson clinical dietitian states that "Alcohol causes damage to the tissues over time, which can lead to changes in the cell's DNA and increased risk for cancer".[20] Another PubMed article reinforces this impact on DNA damage and also describes an increase in "aberrant metabolism" as another possible contributor to creating an environment hospitable to cancer cell reproduction.[20]

  Many dozens of articles on PubMed articulate the risks of drinking alcohol. Quite simply, less is better, and none is best.

  Past articles have cited the positive benefits of alcohol, specifically red wine. In the 1990s, mainstream media frequently trumpeted the benefits of resveratrol, a natural compound found in red wine. The news created such a frenzy that wine sales surged, and people began taking resveratrol supplements. However, the headlines were driven by animal studies not replicated in humans. Dig into this PubMed article to learn how this narrative spread despite relatively little scientific support.[21]

The best arguments for alcohol? It can provide social connections and the mental benefits of those connections. The reality that loneliness is a silent killer might make a drink or two an acceptable risk for you to stay connected to your fellow humans. That's the best defense I can make for alcohol.

While other foods may be carcinogenic, first things first. We must choose our battles, address major concerns first, and double down on what's doable today.

I believe these are major categories worthy of your attention. In relative order of avoidance, I rank them:

1. **Tie for worst:** alcohol and processed sugar (both are poisons)
2. Red meat
3. Dairy

One more guideline for avoiding foods that are unhelpful to your healing: Stay out of the middle of the grocery store, which is home to all the tasty but processed foods that contain a lot of sugar, sodium, and unhealthy preservatives. I can hear the chips calling my name, but I steer clear.

FOODS HELPFUL TO HEALING

Admittedly, I have made wagyu steak and crème brûlée less appetizing. So let's consider tasty foods shown by research to help your body heal—in other words, foods we can use as medicine. I included studies where possible. Candidly, the research on benefits is often sparse—and sometimes even contradictory. Why is that?

1. The concept of food as medicine is widely accepted across many times and places. Yet it can create controversy today.
2. Controlling for a specific food amid all other variables (such as smoking and alcohol consumption) becomes incredibly tricky.
3. Money! Food can't be patented, so spending money to prove its value is usually a non-starter.

There are a couple of key terms you surely have heard and you need to know what they mean:

- **Antioxidant.** A substance that can prevent or delay some types of cell damage. Many fruits and vegetables have ample antioxidants.[22]
- **Inflammation.** The body's response to an irritant. Inflammation causes blood vessels to widen and allow more blood-carrying immune cells to reach the injured tissue, which in severe inflammation can turn the area red and hot.[22]

Below are a few foods I easily incorporated into my diet. If you search online for "antioxidant" or "anti-inflammatory foods," you will find loads more. I do recommend that you work with a dietitian to find the optimum menu for your needs and tastes. Note that too much of any healthy food can have negative side effects, as one friend discovered. After learning about the benefits of walnuts, he started eating multiple servings a day. The result was a severely disrupted digestive system. Trust me, you don't want any more details.

- **Kiwi.** A fruit that I already enjoyed but made a conscious effort to consume more. Studies have found kiwis help prevent oxidative damage to your DNA.[23] Just as some foods negatively impact your DNA, kiwi can help protect it.

- **Berries (strawberry, blueberry, blackberry, and raspberry).** Like kiwi, berries have similar antioxidant properties and protect DNA from damage.[23]

  Another study found that "Edible berries have been demonstrated to extend chemoprevention in cancer primarily of the GI tract as well as breast and to a lesser degree of liver, prostate, pancreas and lung".[23]

- **Tree nuts.** Nuts have a variety of health benefits that go beyond cancer, and eating a diversity of different nuts provides your body with diverse minerals and polyphenols.[23]

- **Coffee (decaf and regular).** Coffee has antioxidant and anti-inflammatory agents that can help boost your immune system as well as reduce inflammation. According to a 2021 report by the American Cancer Institute, coffee and decaf coffee decrease the risk of endometrial and liver cancers and may diminish the risk of mouth, pharynx, larynx, and skin cancers.[23] However, another study found coffee consumption could increase the likelihood of esophageal cancer.[23]

  Although study results are often contradictory, it does seem the majority tilt in favor of coffee as a possible preventative measure. This paper in PubMed links to studies about specific cancers.[23] I personally only drink decaf coffee because after detoxing, my body couldn't handle the caffeine. It made me feel drunk.

- **Tea.** A 2020 meta-analysis found that drinking tea was associated with reduced risk of oral cancer and possible reduced risk of biliary tract, breast, endometrial, and liver cancers.[23]

You can find long lists online of foods that might help you; in fact, so many recommendations that it's impossible to consume all of them. Prioritize what you can easily incorporate into your daily and weekly menus. If you find something you enjoy, stick with it. If you find something unbearable, swap it out. After my diagnosis, I started eating monstrous salads that took an hour to eat. I felt like I was eating the rainforest at every meal, and the unpleasantness was completely unsustainable. I continued to experiment with all kinds of other fruits and vegetables.

One more food resource: Dr. William Li is the bestselling author of *Eat to Beat Disease* and founder of Angiogenesis Foundation. His

YouTube interview with William Howes details healthy foods that heal the body and starve cancer.[24]

GUT BIOME HEALTH

There is more and more research linking our overall health to our gut health. It is generally believed that we have 10 times more microorganisms in our body compared to cells, and most of those microorganisms live in our gut. It is not surprising that we know so little about the 20+ feet between our stomach and colon; we can do an endoscopy to check on our stomach health, and everyone over age 45 knows we can get our colon checked with a colonoscopy. But no similar technique has been developed for our intestines.

The one place you can start is by getting a gut biome test by collecting a stool sample to see all the good and bad bacteria you have in your gut. There are multiple companies offering such a test. Jona was recommended to me (www.Jona.health) but I expect this field will advance rapidly so it's worth researching the current state of things. These tests can be difficult to interpret so I encourage working with a naturopath to understand the results and what to do about them.

Another good resource on this topic is the book *Super Gut* by Dr. William David. He details natural and antibiotic approaches to improving gut health as well as treating SIBO (Small intestinal bacterial overgrowth) and SIFO (Small intestinal fungal overgrowth).

These resources will help you determine what supplements and/or treatments you can do to improve your gut health.

EXERCISE

Although exercise is one of the most important things you can do before, during, and after your diagnosis, I want to keep this brief. What makes sense for one person isn't appealing or appropriate for another; everything depends on your current baseline. If you're bedridden, raising your legs is a great goal. If you're constantly nauseous, walking around the block might be good progress.

Before my diagnosis, I could run 10 miles at a quick pace. Once I got past the acute abdominal pain and nausea, I started to run again.

But I pooped out after a mile and sometimes long before that. Over several months, I slowly increased my distance. Some days I can now complete four miles at a slower pace. Other days I can't do that, but I'm still out there walking and moving my muscles.

For specific cancers, your doctor will advise against extreme exercise or fasting, which can cause cell death via autophagy, a process where the body breaks down existing cells and forms new cells. If you create an extreme environment through rigorous exercise or limited calorie intake, the process of breaking down and reforming can give cancer cells an opportunity to hijack nutrients or mutate in ways that make treatment ineffective.

HEALING YOUR MIND

Talk It Out

While the stigma regarding speaking to a counselor has decreased significantly in recent years, the thought of therapy still might make you queasy. Today's extreme shortage of trained professionals can add a convenient obstacle. Nevertheless, I strongly urge you to give talk therapy a chance. You might need to identify a group practice and meet with a few counselors to find the right fit, but it's worth the effort. Staying within a group practice often minimizes potential insurance headaches.

How do you choose a good therapist? I wish I had a surefire answer, but it's reasonable to start with word of mouth from your community or recommendations from your PCP or oncology office. If someone has availability, ensure that the provider is in-network with your insurance so you don't have to pay out of pocket.

> ***At first, I didn't think I needed a counselor. I didn't see my need at the time because I had no idea of the raw emotions raging inside me until months after my diagnosis.***

They say we go through five stages of grief (denial, anger, bargaining, depression, and acceptance). I was past the point of denial. I admitted I was facing one hell of a problem. But I buried my anger to the point I didn't even know it was there. If you read my story in the first part of this book, you know I experienced an acute event that forced me to recognize my need. After that event, it was blazingly obvious I needed a guide through this process.

I wanted to move forward quickly, so I started "dating" multiple therapists at once. I worked with an online therapist, added an online peer counselor, and then met with an in-person counselor. The online therapist was trained in a specific protocol that didn't fit my situation, and that person's sincere attempts to customize to my needs didn't really work. I greatly benefited from my peer counselor's help working through specific issues. While each was valuable, in the end, I found the dynamic with the face-to-face counselor best suited me.

Meditation/Prayer

Meditation and/or prayer can be an enormous help as you emotionally navigate this very challenging time. If you have never meditated, it can be challenging to figure out where to start. There are many apps out there (Calm, Headspace, Waking Up, Insight Timer, and more) and each has supporters and detractors. I gravitated toward the paid version of Insight Timer, which is where I found a 10-day meditation by Giovanni Dienstmann titled "What Meditation Type is Best for You." I was introduced to a variety of meditations and discovered what resonated with me. It's common at the start to lose focus, but like learning a language or instrument, you get better with practice. In general, I recommend meditating first thing in the morning or as the last thing you do before you go to sleep.

Prayer can be another important part of your healing journey. As a believer, people asked me how I reconciled meditation and prayer. I noted earlier in my story that I didn't find a conflict, and my faith made room to combine the two. I often prayed after meditating.

#PEP

Prayer, Energy and Positivity! Who and how many people you inform of your diagnosis is a highly personal decision. Whatever the size or shape of that group, I strongly believe each person should contribute PEP to your cause. If someone doesn't bring one or more elements of PEP to help with your healing, you might choose to limit your interactions with that person. You need to see PEP in their face and hear PEP in their voice. Anything less can knock you out of a positive mindset and your belief that healing is possible.

That said, give people a moment to get on board. Explain what you need and how they can help you in your fight. So many people give up when they hear their diagnosis, but you're not one of them. Healing your body is a long and arduous road, and you need every bit of help other humans can give you. Can that person help with prayer? Or energy? Or positivity?

I believe we are all fundamentally connected, and if you openly request PEP from fellow humans, they will answer and help you on your road to healing. In my quest for healing, I felt the more the merrier, which soon compelled me to go public with my diagnosis. While there are obvious trade-offs to containing a diagnosis within a small group, I knew in my gut that my cancer had advanced, and I needed a ton of help to heal my body. The outpouring I have received leaves no doubt in my mind that these humans all play a part in remission. I believe I can help you too, which is why I decided to write this book.

I'm sending PEP to you and your family as you look to navigate this challenging time.

PRACTICALITIES

Leave of Work

Be aware that if you work as an exempt employee, that is, you receive a salary, you could be eligible for paid leave. Every employer has different benefits, but it's common to get up to three months a year at a specified percentage of your salary as well as the safety of staying on the company's health plan, which is critical as you receive treatment.

If taking leave is at all possible from a financial perspective, I strongly encourage you to take advantage of this benefit. You need your mind primarily focused on healing your body, and if you're worried about the next deliverable at work, that stress obviously isn't ideal.

A leave requires paperwork, but your oncology office should be well-versed in this area and be able to complete it on your behalf. As an aside, they might even be able to get you out of jury duty if you happen to be summoned while receiving treatment. A "friend" told me that.

Containing Cost

Paying for treatment can add to an already significant challenge. A few approaches to consider:

- **Subsidies.** It's possible your oncology clinic can help to subsidize your drug or pay for it entirely. This is more likely if the drug is newer to the market or you're using it for an off-label purpose (not its intended use per its regulatory approval) because the oncology clinic might be able to access a discount from the drug manufacturer.

- **Costplusdrugs.com.** This is an online pharmacy founded by Mark Cuban and Alex Oshmyansky with the goal of offering low-cost, high-quality drugs directly to the consumer with complete price transparency. They sell prescription drugs at their cost from the manufacturer plus 15% for their margin and $5 for shipping. That's it. The biggest challenge is that the selection of drugs might not include your medication. It's worth checking to see if they sell your medication.

- **Out-of-pocket maximum.** More and more providers attempt to collect the patient's responsibility upfront, sometimes not even allowing you to check in for appointments. Knowing the dollars remaining before you meet your out-of-pocket maximum can be critical in avoiding paying upfront charges you later need to get refunded, a process that can become its own nightmare. Tracking all this is likely too much for patients in the thick of treatment, so enlist a close family member or friend to manage this on your behalf. I'm still trying to reclaim $500 from a CT scan over 15 months ago.

When You Can't Speak For Yourself

An "advance directive" is a legal document that states your desires for medical care in the event you are no longer able to communicate and make these decisions yourself. A "living will" is a type of advance directive focused on end-of-life treatment. These documents are essential for everyone, especially anyone dealing with a cancer diagnosis.

80% of Americans endorse having an advance directive, yet only 1 in 3 has one.[25]

Why is there an enormous gap? Speaking from personal experience, it's incredibly painful to complete. Maybe for the first time ever, you're forced to think about your own mortality, a topic almost no one willingly considers. I didn't. Not until I stared down the barrel of a rare Stage 4 cancer diagnosis.

Consider these questions you will need to confront:

- Do I want life-sustaining treatments? Does that include CPR? Does that include being on a ventilator?
- Do I want artificial nutrition and hydration if these are the main treatments keeping me alive?
- Do I want relief from pain even if it hastens my death?
- How might my medical condition affect my family?
- If I were permanently unconscious and unable to speak for myself, I would want (finish the sentence).
- When do I no longer want my life prolonged?

You can't just bang out those answers like a quick text. They require significant thought. The last question really stumped me because if there's a chance, even a statistically small probability, do I really not want to seize that opportunity for life?

I forced myself to think practically: When I am unable to do (fill in the blank), I no longer want lifesaving efforts. My test? "When I'm no longer able to understand my wife's scrapbooks or recognize the people in them, I no longer want to be here."

If there is nothing that is highly likely to change the above, I am done. If you quibbled that "highly likely" isn't specific enough, I would agree. But there are limits to what we can foresee and decide.

Note: Just like "Standard Metabolic Panels" aren't standard, neither are advance directives. Each state has its template, some of which require notarization. Certain advance directives don't require you to answer these questions but assign specific decisions to your agent.

Don't settle for handing off responsibility if that's all your state requires. The more detail you can provide for your family, the more you can define a clear and simple test of your desires—the better.

Another thing to consider: How would you answer these questions if there is a chance of full recovery (like after a traumatic car crash) versus you're near the end of life (cancer, a terminal illness, or simply old age)? Let's revisit a few questions again. Imagine you're a family member having to answer on your behalf:

- Do I want lifesaving treatments? Does that include CPR? Does that include being on a ventilator?
- Do I want to be kept alive on a ventilator after a difficult surgery?
- Do I want to be kept alive on a ventilator when the doctor says I have weeks or days to live?
- How long do I want to be kept alive on a ventilator? One day? A week? A month?

You very quickly see all kinds of gray in these decisions. If you don't take the time to turn the gray to black and white, it falls to your loved ones to make those agonizing calls. Please take the guesswork and guilt out of decision-making!

Do this before you get sick. Frankly, put this book down, download the form for your state, and get started. When my mom was diagnosed with Stage 4 lung cancer, she wasn't cognitively present for large stretches of time. During her coherent moments, I talked about getting an advance directive in place. She didn't want to touch the topic. I was saddened by her decision, but I also didn't want to push her during the few good moments we had left with her.

As mom's cognition left her and her time became shorter, I could see the burden this put on my dad. It was like he was emotionally carrying the weight of a grand piano on his back. Am I really doing what she wants? Does she want to keep fighting? Would she be okay if we moved her to hospice and she stopped taking the one drug that might extend her life? Should we do hospice at home? These questions weighed on him every single day.

Luckily for us, mom became coherent near the end and made the decision to transition to hospice. It still feels like a gift she was able to give my dad in her final days. In this instance, we got lucky. But an advance directive would have removed the guesswork and made an incredibly painful situation a little less awful, knowing we were honoring her wishes.

Financial Matters

Wills and Trusts for Probate States, Community Property vs Common Law states

Having an advanced directive will hopefully minimize the emotional decisions at the end. Having a will, and potentially a trust, will help minimize financial decisions. This topic gets very complicated very quickly, so I won't go into detail other than this: Understand your state's probate process. If you have significant assets, having a will might not be enough, whereas having a trust could make the transition of assets dramatically easier. The state of California is a prime example. Depending on your state of residence, your assets could be stuck in probate for years, something you clearly want to avoid for your loved ones. Just as in the case of an advance directive, do this and do it now.

Godspeed, my friend!

I hope you have found this how-to information helpful. I'm grateful you have traveled this journey with me. I want you to know there's more to my story.

END NOTES

17 **National Center for Biotechnology Information (NCBI).** *Current Evidence and Directions for Intermittent Fasting During Cancer Chemotherapy.* Journal article. https://www.ncbi.nlm.nih.gov/pmc/articles/PMC8970823/

18 **Wikipedia.** *Naturopathy.* Reference article. https://en.wikipedia.org/wiki/Naturopathy

19 **National Center for Biotechnology Information (NCBI).** *Dairy products intake and cancer mortality risk: a meta-analysis of 11 population-based cohort studies.* Journal article. https://www.ncbi.nlm.nih.gov/pmc/articles/PMC5073921/

20 **National Institutes of Health / PubMed; MD Anderson Cancer Center.** *Research articles and clinical guidance examining red meat, alcohol, and other dietary factors associated with cancer risk.*
https://pubmed.ncbi.nlm.nih.gov/34455534/
https://pubmed.ncbi.nlm.nih.gov/37849565/
https://pubmed.ncbi.nlm.nih.gov/28805741/
https://www.mdanderson.org/cancerwise/5-foods-and-drinks-linked-to-cancer.h00-159623379.html

21 **National Center for Biotechnology Information (NCBI).** *Resveratrol and Wine: An Overview of Thirty Years in the Digital News.* Review article. https://www.ncbi.nlm.nih.gov/pmc/articles/PMC9740773/

22 **MedlinePlus; National Center for Biotechnology Information (NCBI).** *Medical reference resources explaining antioxidants and the inflammatory response.*
https://medlineplus.gov/antioxidants.html
https://www.ncbi.nlm.nih.gov/books/NBK279298/

23 **National Center for Biotechnology Information (NCBI); American Institute for Cancer Research (AICR).** *Selected research and guidance on diet-related factors and cancer risk.*
https://pubmed.ncbi.nlm.nih.gov/11588897/
https://www.ncbi.nlm.nih.gov/pmc/articles/PMC5187535/
https://www.ncbi.nlm.nih.gov/pmc/articles/PMC8468443/
https://www.aicr.org/cancer-prevention/food-facts/coffee/
https://pubmed.ncbi.nlm.nih.gov/36067583/
https://www.ncbi.nlm.nih.gov/pmc/articles/PMC9916720/

24 **YouTube.** *Video presentation on diet, cancer prevention, and metabolic health.* Video presentation. https://youtu.be/jdsn8t7mCkQ

25 **National Institutes of Health / PubMed.** *Characteristics of Patients With Existing Advance Directives: Evaluating Motivations Around Advance Care Planning.* Research article. https://pubmed.ncbi.nlm.nih.gov/28925295/

EPILOGUE

THE JOURNEY

A friend once said that when people ask him about Chris's cancer diagnosis, he says this: "Chris went on a deeply personal journey. The cancer forced him to find himself, be true to himself, and with God's love, ultimately become healed."

As I reflect on the last two years, this description resonates with me. I stared at death three times, yet thanks to God, I'm still alive today. Reading this far has given you a front-row seat to what I went through. As I wrap up my writing, I wanted to pause for a moment and distill my most important realizations.

On the fateful day of my diagnosis, one of my medical advisors gave me my first piece of advice: "Mindset is everything." I have taken those words to heart ever since.

It hasn't been easy. Pain kills optimism and opens the door to dark thoughts. Make no mistake, I have had thousands of dark thoughts over the last two years. Yet on balance they have been merely passing visitors in my mind as I looked to regain a positive mindset.

Optimism returns.

Optimism is resilient.

And if you let it, optimism can carry the day.

You must believe something is possible for it to be possible, so at a minimum, start there. **Believe you can be healed.**

In a nod to Ted Lasso, our daughter Emma built this sign out of Legos and placed it near our ceiling, tilted and all. I touch it after every workout and repeat, "My body is healed."

I firmly believe in the mind-body connection—that what we think impacts our body for better or worse. I'm therefore very careful with my words and avoid saying words like "my" in front of the "C" word. How can it go away if I'm always trying to claim it? I avoid saying the "C" word whenever possible. Given that, I try to follow this quote:

> *"Don't speak negatively about yourself, even as a joke.*
> *Your body doesn't know the difference. Words are energy*
> *and they cast spells; that's why it's called spelling.*
> *Change the way you speak about yourself,*
> *and you can change your life."*
> Bruce Lee

YOU INDEED HAVE AGENCY

When the "C" word is uttered, your life can feel like it's spinning out of control and you're merely along for the ride. I hope this book has challenged you to reject passivity as the default option. You can take the wheel.

Remember, you indeed have agency over many things. Allow me to remind you what I said back in chapter 2:

1. You can accept the recommended treatment plan or opt for a different approach. Yes, there will be immense pressure from physicians, your family, and friends, but this is your body and your life. Make the decision you feel is right, and don't acquiesce and die on account of politeness!
2. You can decide to make changes to your diet.
3. You can decide if you want to adjust your approach to exercise.
4. You can decide to address potential emotional issues from your past.
5. You can decide your mindset and how you are going to think.
6. You can decide to adopt mindfulness practices such as meditation or prayer.
7. You can decide if there are ways to reduce stress in your life.
8. You can decide if you want to explore alternative therapies like intravenous vitamin C, acupuncture, reiki, Ayervedic approaches, or others.
9. You can decide to explore natural supplements that could boost your immune system.
10. You can decide to explore off-label drug use as another low-cost way to treat your body.
11. You can decide how to breathe. As silly as it sounds, I focused on changing my breathing. Several times a day, an alarm on my phone reminds me to pause just to breathe. My daughters laugh. I say, "More belly, more better!"

As evidenced above, there is much you can choose to do for your happiness and healing. My morning meditation helps reinforce this belief in me. As Wayne Dyer says, "I know in each moment I am free to decide."

GIVE UP CONTROL OF THE OUTCOME

When the cancer came back, I tried to get in the same mindset as before. We would throw everything at the illness, visualize my healing happening, and get back to remission. However, a funny thing happened after a surprise hospitalization drove home the point that I have no idea what the future holds, much less the next 24 hours. And that's okay.

I'm listening to God, I'm listening to my body, and I can conceive of multiple ways my body will become healed. Do I spend time visualizing by which mechanism, or where, how, or when it will happen? Absolutely not. I have faith that as I listen and follow God's path, I will become healed exactly when, where, and how it's supposed to happen.

At first, you might think this is crazy. How can I let go like that? But once I did, I felt liberated. I no longer spend countless brain cycles wondering. No more hours in bed reasoning through the odds of which path is most likely. No more family discussions about permutations and possibilities for healing. Just extreme optimism and faith that healing will happen.

As I noted above, I never want to discount how much agency you have. But do what you can— then know you've done your part. Don't waste a minute worrying about things beyond your control. Instead, sit in the present, savor the moments, and your life will be richer for it.

There's an exchange in the background audio of my favorite pinball game, Star Trek: The Next Generation. It goes something like this:

Captain Picard: "What is our exact destination?"
Lieutenant Commander Data: "Unknown, Captain. Unknown."

Exactly how it should be!

MY PURPOSE AS A HEALTHCARE LEADER

I have spent more than 15 years in healthcare leadership. Intellectually, I have grown to understand that the system is badly broken. After watching my mom pass and enduring my own two-year journey, I now feel its brokenness viscerally. In rereading my own words, I'm still astonished at how hard everything was—tasks as basic as getting a prescription, a scan, or even an appointment. Given the constant barriers faced by cancer patients, I wonder how anyone survives. I'm privileged with my knowledge, connections, and financial means to afford the standard options and several more. Most people aren't so lucky. How many people are scared, alone, and unsure what to do next?

I wrote this book to help those people. While I hope it delivers on this promise, it's obvious to me that more must be done.

We can't simply duct-tape the current healthcare infrastructure and hope human experiences and outcomes improve. We need to completely reengineer the system.

To create permanent and far-reaching change, we need to begin by understanding what "good" looks like from the patient's point of view. What the rest of us think is important matters little compared to that.

Whenever entrepreneurs come up with an idea, their first questions are "What is the voice of the customer?" and "Will they buy it?" Ironically, people running the healthcare system don't have a clear view of what the customer wants. Most lack the firsthand experience of being a patient of a serious illness. To address this knowledge gap, I founded the nonprofit **FixTheSystemOrDieTrying.org.** My first goal is to collect patient stories—both good and bad—so we can fully and accurately inform the healthcare system what good looks like from the patient's point of view. Crazy, right?

If you have journeyed with me this far, please take a few minutes to visit the site below and share your stories. What you say will help provide input on how we can change the healthcare system for the better. For as long as I'm breathing on this Earth, this is now my purpose.

Thank you—and PEP to you!

"Big" Chris

Scan to visit
fixthesystemordietrying.org

ACKNOWLDGEMENTS

My wife, my rock, my love, Jing. Words can't do justice to what you have done for me to be able to be alive and write these words.

My girls, Emma and Jasmine. I'm proud of the strong women you already are. I cannot wait to see what positive dent you make in the universe.

Kevin Johnson, my book coach. This was a labor of love. Thank you for helping craft it.

Richard Dodson, my book producer, who brought the book to life.

My medical advisors, who were there to debrief after every medical visit. Andy Greenfield, Jerry Maccioli, Alex Pastuszak, and Brad Stewart.

My friends Dusty Durden and Mike Pozzi, who were there the entire time, always supporting me.

My friends Blake and Beth Baron who came to rescue me after my psychotic event.

My Western Medicine team, led by Dr. Daniel Pease, Dr. Jay Podaly, Dr. Jonathan Trent, and Dr. Andrew Blakely.

My Eastern Medicine team of Michael Broffman and Nikki Vanecek.

To the Life Raft Group, which provided us with critical information along the way.

My worldwide PEP team. Not sure I would be here without all of you. The positivity, the energy, and the prayers—I felt them. They lifted me up and gave me the strength to keep pushing.

I love you all and am eternally grateful for the roles you played to get me here.

IN GRADITUDE OF

Naman Aggarwal
Amar
Ryan Armbruster
Shoib Bajaj
Matt Barrett
Ling Becker
Conor Beardsley
David Berry
John Broderick
Michael Brousseau
Jeffrey Burr
Christopher Cahill
Erica Neubert Campbell
Nu Chan
Claire Cochrane
Chris Comenos
Steve Cuff
Vincent Darmali
Joe Delgado
Nick Doty
Gilbert Drozdow
Dusty Durden
Erlendur Eiriksson
Charles Fan
Rob Fannon
Jen Farmer
Pascal Ferzli
Crissy Flake
Erica Foskett
Brenda Fox
Jenn Gilchrist
Gary L. Goldsmith
Tom Goldsmith
Yahaira Gomez
Andrew Greenfield
Bill Guptail
Andy Guttman
Rick Hardy
Tommy Harke
Michael Heller
Robert Hood
Laura Irwin
Justin Jacobsen
Ricardo Jorge
Tyler Kargman
Chirag Katbamna
Brandon Klein
Sabita Lahiri
Julius Lai
Eyal Lavin
JC LeBraud
Jeanne Leising
Daniel Lima
Brad Logan
Lara Lorenz
David Mace
Scott Mancuso
Marc Marple
Ron Massey
Joe McManus
Anita Todd Messal
Mark
Matt Miller
Rabih Modad
Richard J Montwill
Megan Mornard
Manuj Naman
Deb Napolski
Patrick Nelli
Fran Newman

Andrew Ninh
Chris Nelson
Jordan Oelschlager
Keith Oelschlager
Jim Opfinger
Kyle Pak
Mark Panfel
Al Pita
Roger Plasterer
Rob Posner
Michael Pozzi
Anna Plunkett
Marshall Preston
Anoop Raman
Jon Rathbun
Brooks Rawlin
Jim Rensberger
Michael Rensberger
Kara Roncin
Nicholas Sacco
Jacob Sack
Mark Sechrist
Mark and Pinata Sessoms
Kari Severson Snaza
Mike and Janet Soohoo
Paul Steen
Alan Struthers
Jon Szafranski
Kurt Tamaru
Tara
Tina Taylor
Susan Teal
Bill Trubeck
Marjorie Veiga
Sara Velez
Alexis Williams
Joe Wagner
Justin Ward
Heather Wasielewski-Lopez
John Way
Robert Weiler
Tom Weiler
Chris Weinstein
Adam and Sarah Wexler
Julie Woodward
Tom Ziesmann

IN HONOR OF

Anyone Facing Cancer
Kimberly Barr
Elise Berg
Dip Buddy
Yip Chan
Rose Nan-Ping Chen
Elaine DeAngelis
Jeannette Fossion Dietz
Margaret Durden
Erla Maria Erlendsdottir
Mama Frita
Kay Furst
Joe Gill
Kathy Goldsmith
Lloyd Goldsmith
Mildred Goldsmith
Gung Gung
Nidish C. Gupta
Dipak & Prafulla Katbamna
Ellickal Isaac Jose
JC LeBraud
Pearl Marie Leuty
Geneva Logan
Maia
Barbara Mace
Erik Medeby
Norma Meyer
Mary Murley
Linda Gibson Preston
Ronald P. Pozzi Jr.
Ryan Reinhardt
Wendy Robinson
Sanna
Frank V. Sacco
Heather Schwartzbauer
David Szafranski
Alyssa Stevens
Velez Family
Earnestine “Tina” Walker
Julie Woodward

ABOUT THE AUTHOR

Cancer survivor, Girl Dad, Author, Healthcare Change Agent

Chris Goldsmith is a seasoned healthcare executive with over 15 years of experience in operations, strategy, and leadership within the healthcare industry. He has held multiple executive roles including Co-Founder, CEO, President, and COO. He has seen where the system has helped many humans but also where it has dramatically failed, including his own fight to heal his body from cancer.

He holds a Master of Business Administration from INSEAD in France and a Bachelor of Science in Environmental Engineering from Duke University. Residing in Minneapolis with his family, he is deeply committed to fixing the healthcare system or die trying.

APPENDIX

In case you want to see pictures of what was removed.

Image 1: Appendix with tumor growth

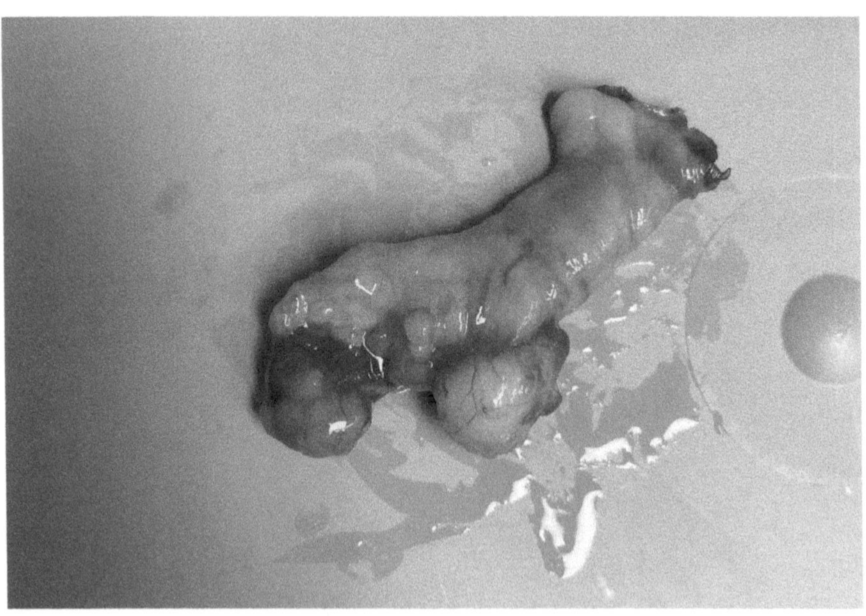

Image 2: Primary tumor with small intestine

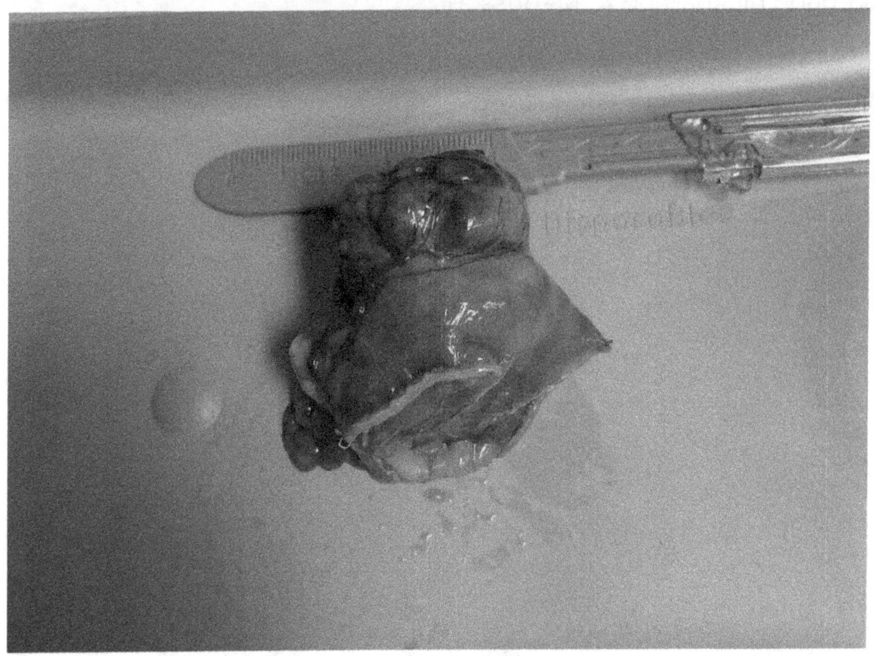

Image 3: Example of one of the 80 peritoneal tumors

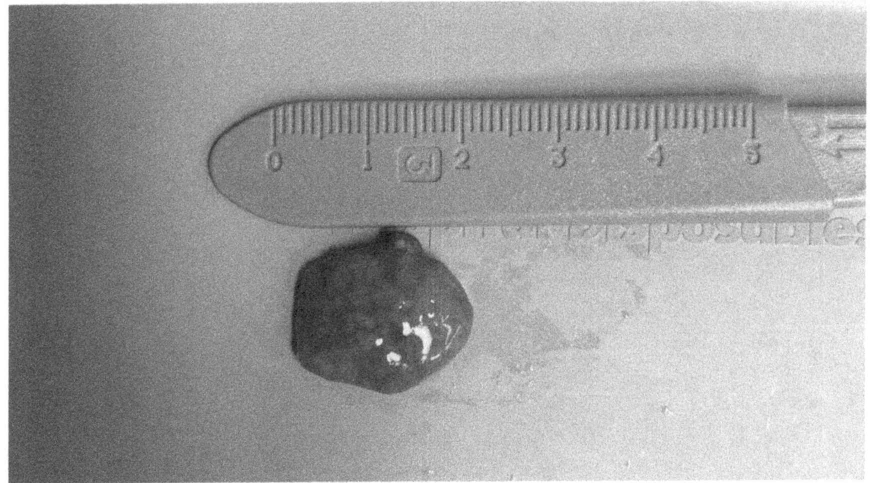

Image 4: The tumor removed from my pelvis, a growth so ugly the surgeon nicknamed it "Medusa."

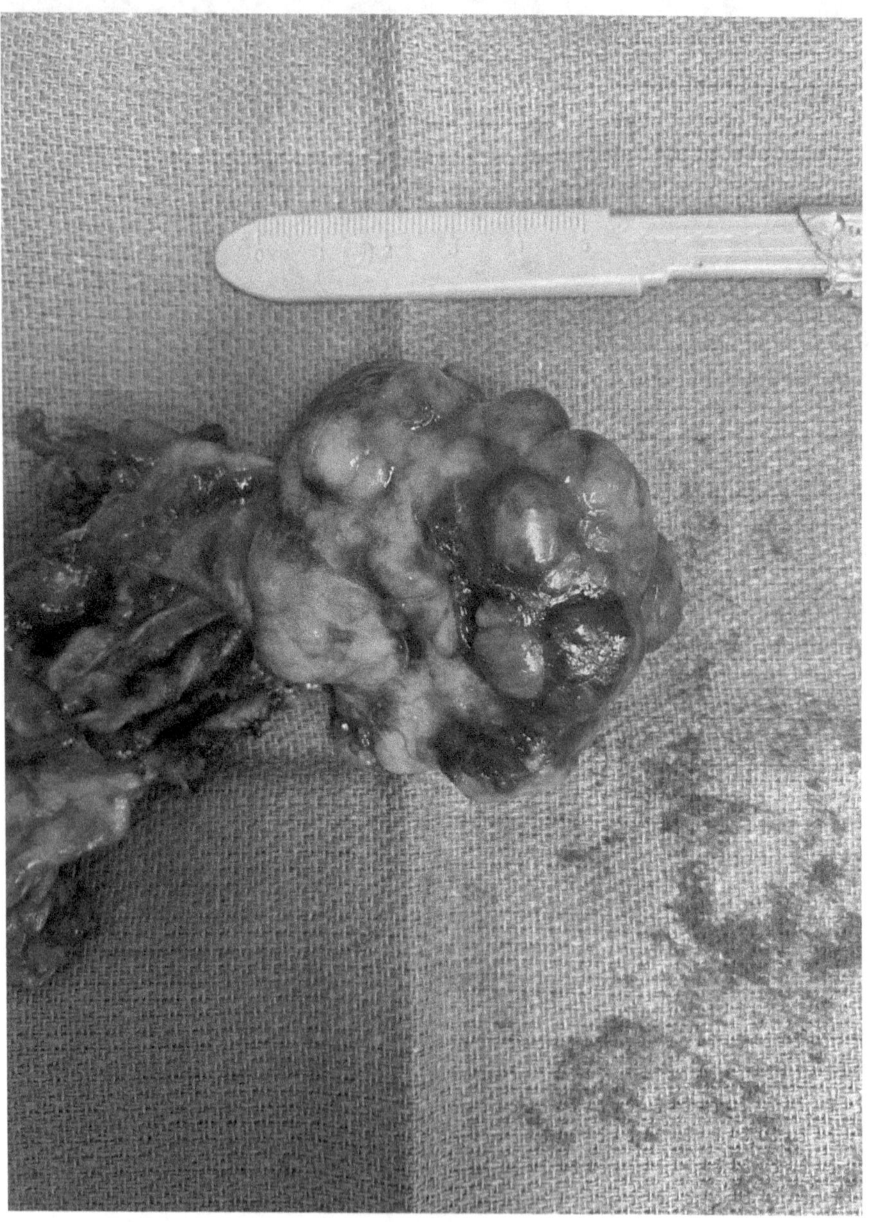

Image 5: The incision, still with staples

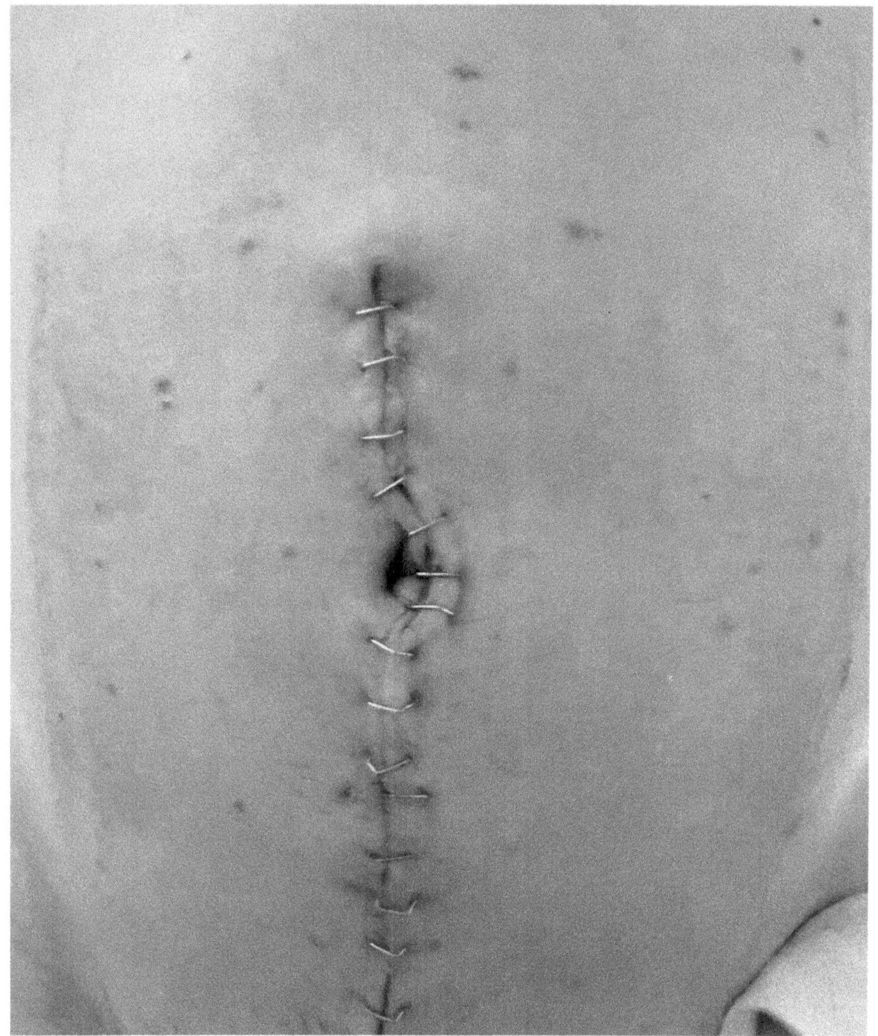

www.ingramcontent.com/pod-product-compliance
Lightning Source LLC
LaVergne TN
LVHW050538160826
845677LV00011B/2090

* 9 7 9 8 9 9 4 5 2 1 3 1 1 *